WINDSOR PARK

A History of the Home of Linfield FC & Northern Ireland

By JOE CASSELLS

First published in Great Britain in 2022

Copyright © Joe Cassells 2022

Published by Victor Publishing - victorpublishing.co.uk

Joe Cassells has asserted his right under the Copyright, Designs and Patents Act 1988 to be identified as the author of this work.

All rights reserved. No part of this publication may be reproduced, distributed, or transmitted in any form or by any means, including photocopying, recording, or other electronic or mechanical methods, without the prior written permission of the author.

ISBN: 9798425751782

Victor
PUBLISHING
www.victorpublishing.co.uk

WINDSOR PARK

A History of the Home of Linfield FC & Northern Ireland

By JOE CASSELLS

Contents

1. The beginnings of Linfield 7
2. Ballynafeigh and the 1888-89 FA cup run 13
3. Ulsterville and homeless (1889 – 1895) 19
4. Balmoral ground, Myrtlefield (1896 – 1905) 29
5. Windsor Park purchase and development 1904 – 1910 33
6. Turnstiles - 'Ellison's Rush Preventive Turnstiles' 55
7. 1920s - Football, boxing, athletics, rugby and speedway 59
8. 1930s - Archibald Leitch's grand stand 71
9. 1940s - The post World War Two boom 87
10. 1950s - Expansion plans, Midgley Park and floodlights 97
11. 1960s - Reducing the capacity 113
12. 1970s - Troubled times 119
13. 1980s - A new stand for Windsor 125
14. 1990s - Farewell to The Kop 137
15. 2000s - Decline and renewal 143
16. 2010s - A National Stadium at Windsor Park 151
17. 2020s - A stadium fit for the 21st Century 161

Acknowledgements 169

Selected biography 171

About the author 173

1

The beginnings of Linfield

The game of "football" – the activity where young men kicked an object of some sort towards a "goal" – had existed in one form or another in Ireland and elsewhere since at least the 16th century. The Irish Sunday Observance Act of 1695 sought to prohibit 'hurling, commoning, foot-ball playing'.

"Association football" – that is, organised football games played to a set of agreed rules – is generally thought to have commenced in Ireland in the 1870's, with the first recorded game played by members of the Ulster Cricket Club at its ground at Prospect, south Belfast in front of some spectators on 11th December 1875. On the 24th October 1878 the two Scottish teams Caledonians and Queen's Park played a demonstration game at the same ground. That match was partly organised by Belfast businessman John McAlery, who in 1879 formed the Cliftonville club in Belfast. The following year, the Irish Football Association was established to organise, govern and promote the game. The IFA was the fourth football association to be formed in the world, following those established in England, Scotland and Wales.

The inaugural Irish Cup – organised on a knockout basis, and modelled on the world's oldest football competition, the Football Association's Challenge Cup that had been played for in England since 1871/72 – was played in 1881 with seven teams entering, Moyola Park winning the first final by defeating Cliftonville 1-0 on 9th April 1881.

The IFA quickly adopted the Scotch rule book, and in 1882 an International Board, consisting of delegates from each of the four 'home' UK associations, was formed with the express purpose of ensuring a common set of rules for competitions. The first Ireland international match, a friendly against England, took place at Bloomfield in Belfast in February 1882.

Belfast in the 1880's was a rapidly developing industrial centre. The linen trade played a pivotal role in Belfast's social and economic development, and the manufacture of linen was the catalyst that allowed it to grow from a town into the region's pre-eminent city. It grew most rapidly during the 1860s, and by the end of the 19th century Belfast was the linen capital of the world.

Initially linen production was a domestic activity on farms, but the industrial revolution brought mechanisation to the process and the method of "wet spinning" brought about a proliferation of spinning mills. People flocked from rural areas into Belfast to work in the new spinning mills, and by 1871 there were 78 mills in the region with a workforce of 43,000.

The bulk of linen manufacturing was carried on in the west and south of the city, where the Ulster Spinning Company had established the Linfield Mill in the mid-1800s. It was reputedly the largest and best equipped linen mill of its kind in Belfast.

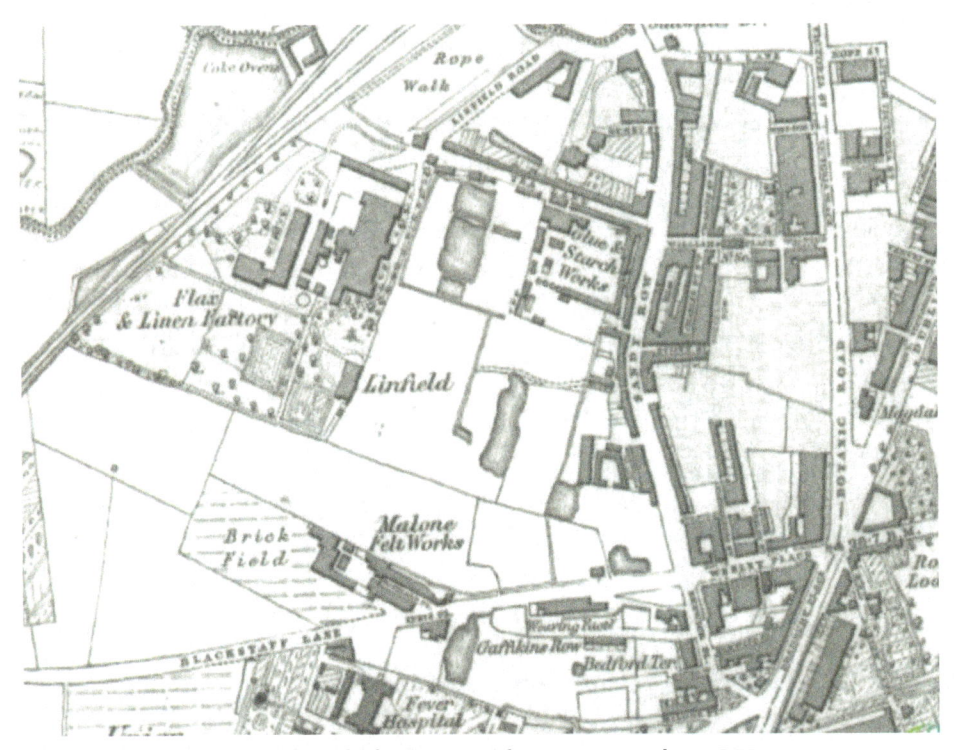

Map showing the site of the Linfield Flax & Linen Factory circa 1860s

The Linfield Mill was situated in the Sandy Row district of south Belfast. The name Sandy Row derived from the sandbank which abutted the road that followed the high-water mark resulting from the flow of the tidal waters of the Lagan River estuary. For over two thousand years, the road along the sandbank was the principal thoroughfare leading south from Carrickfergus.

King William, Prince of Orange was reputed to have passed along the Row on his way to fight the Battle of the Boyne in 1690. In the 1880's the area was heavily industrialised and consisted of small terraced houses for the mostly working class employees of the various mills and foundries in the city.

The populace of the area was overwhelmingly Protestant/Unionist, and there were occasional tensions and riots between residents and those from the nearby, Catholic/Nationalist, Pound Loney (Falls) district.

WINDSOR PARK - A History of the Home of Linfield FC & Northern Ireland

Football proved to be a popular sport for players and spectators, rivalling the established sports of rugby and cricket, and in the latter part of 1885 workers at the Linfield Mill sought to establish their own association football team.

Bob McClurg, an employee, led a deputation to ask directors permission to form a team and to use the spare ground at the back of the mill as a pitch. This was granted in March 1886 and the company offered the facilities of the dining hall for the players to change.

Newspapers of the summer of 1886 record the activities of the Linfield Athletics cricket team, and the participation by individuals of Linfield Athletics in cycling and running races, so it is assumed that association football was only one of a number of sporting activities undertaken by the employees of the Linfield Mill, with the support of the mill owners.

Linfield Mill, just before its closure in 1963

Linfield Mill (1886 – 1889)

As the new team began training in the summer of 1886, it was initially decided to limit membership to the employees of the mill. It soon became evident, however, that if they were to be successful then others would have to be welcomed into the fold. Soon Linfield were ready for their first competitive game and as there was as yet no official league, a friendly was arranged against the Distillery club, another Belfast side.

The Distillery club had formed in 1880 and, like Linfield, owed their origins to a Belfast industry – in their case the Dunville & Co Whiskey distillery, located a few hundred yards from the Linfield Mill. The Distillery team were the favourites to win the match, having won the Irish Cup three years in a row from 1884 to 1886.

With the Linfield Athletic players kitted out in blue and white striped shirts, the local newspaper the Belfast Telegraph announced the first match to be played at the Mill:

GRAND FOOTBALL MATCH.

OPENING OF NEW FOOTBALL GROUNDS AT LINFIELD.

DISTILLERY v. LINFIELD ATHLETES.

THE above Clubs will Meet for the first Match of the Season, at LINFIELD, on SATURDAY Next, September 11th.
Kick-off at 3.15 sharp.
Entrance to Grounds by Front Gate of Linfield Mill (Linfield Road).
Admission, 3d.   Ladies Free.   509

Advert for Linfield Athletics' first match, 1886

'These clubs will meet tomorrow, in a friendly match, the Distillery having very kindly consented to open the new football grounds of the Linfield Athletics, situated at the rear of Linfield Mill, and, if the weather be at all favourable, a well-contested game may be witnessed, as the junior club has been in hard training for some time, and may give their veteran opponents an obstinate resistance.'

On the same day of this first match at the Mill, the Linfield Athletics cricket team were scheduled to play Ulster, at grounds at Ballynafeigh in the south of the city. However, the Belfast News Letter report of the football match suggests the weather may have intervened:

'Distillery v. Linfield Athletics (Association Rules)

The new football grounds of the latter club were opened on Saturday last. The weather was not at all propitious, and the periodical showers throughout the day caused the ground to be damp and slippery, nevertheless the spectators that braved the storm were awarded a fair exhibition of the dribbling game. The result of the match proved quite a surprise to the spectators, as it was thought throughout to be a walkover for the Distillery: however the match eventually resulted in a win for the Linfield by 6 goals to 5.'

Whilst there was no league in 1886 to compete in, Linfield entered the Irish Football Association Challenge Cup in October, being drawn against Mercantile College:

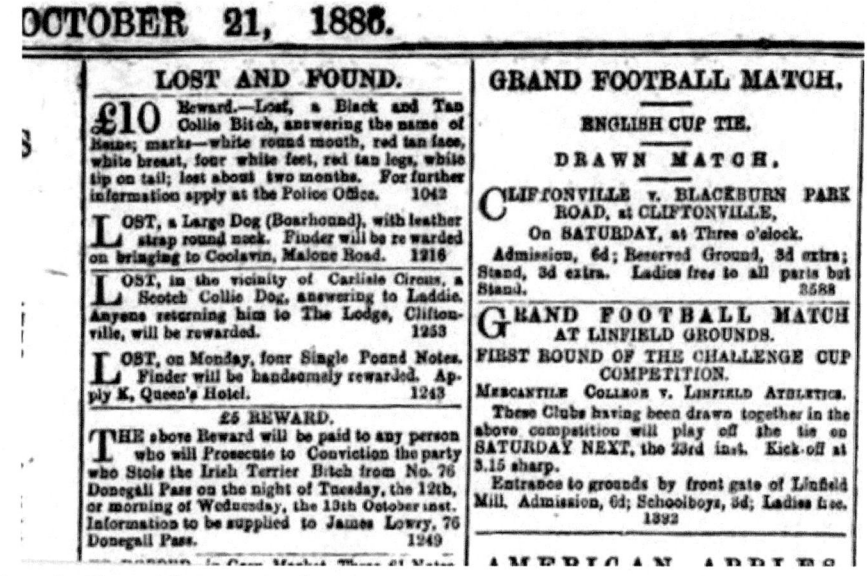

Advert for first Irish Cup match, 1886

The admission charges of 6d (3d schoolboys) and ladies free were relatively modest, and complied with the IFA's ruling in 1884 that teams entering its competitions should have access to a pitch to which entrance could be controlled. Linfield won the match 10-2.

Other fixtures at The Mill were arranged on a friendly basis, though few clubs left with a victory; they didn't like playing there and Distillery's Olphie Stanfield complained that the pitch was too short and the goalposts should not be placed hard against the factory wall. The pitch also had a slight incline.

Belfast continued to expand, and in 1888 was granted city status by Queen Victoria. As the city grew, so did the interest in football, and spectators turned out for Linfield matches in large numbers. A game at the Mill on 15th September 1888 against Distillery attracted 'almost 2,000 persons – the greatest number ever assembled on the Linfield ground.' Later that month it was noted that 'their ground on the Linfield Road has recently been drained and otherwise improved.'

The following month, the Committee established to run the Linfield Athletic team were commended for the improvements they had made to the ground prior to an Irish Cup match against fellow Belfast team Cliftonville: 'The Committee of the Linfield Club have made great improvements to their ground for this important match, chief among these being the laying off of a "reserve" portion of the ground, while a number of seats and foot rails have been provided for the accommodation of ladies, &c.'

Linfield won the match 3-0 and the 'immense crowd – and certainly a greater has never been seen on a football field in Belfast – cheered both teams lustily.' The crowd was described as standing round the ropes eleven and twelve deep, and almost £60 was taken at the gate, or rather, the door. 'The seats and foot rails provided were largely taken advantage of by the ladies, who were present, in great force. ... From the peculiar size of the ground and the position of the goals, all the advantage of the ground is on the side of the home team; and critics generally agree that playing at home is worth a couple of goals to Linfield'.

Admission that day was 9d and 6d (schoolboys 3d, ladies free), and the reported gate suggests a minimum crowd of 1,600 but probably many more given the reduced entrance fees for boys and free entry for the ladies.

Certainly, Linfield enjoyed the 'home' advantage of playing at the Mill (which in later years was recalled as being known by the slightly more appealing name 'The Meadow'), and the available records show the team winning all but 5 of the 31 matches played. Those 31 games included a friendly against a 'foreign' team – Neilston, a mill town in Renfrewshire, just outside Glasgow.

2

Ballynafeigh

and the 1888-89 FA cup run

Although the ground at Ballynafeigh, known as the Ulster Cricket Ground, was never officially Linfield's 'home' ground, the team played a series of important matches there.

The ground, situated in the Ormeau area of south Belfast, was the home of the Ulster Club from 1879. Originally a cricket club, a formal football club was formed in 1877, playing mainly rugby. The ground included a pavilion with terraces in front, and two reserved areas.

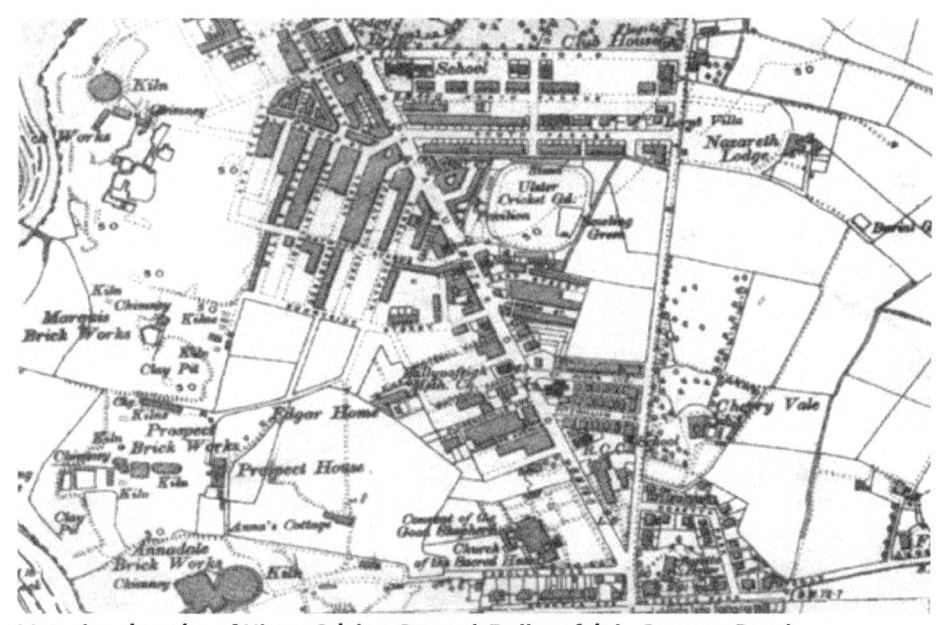

Map showing site of Ulster Cricket Ground, Ballynafeigh, Ormeau Road

Ireland's second home international match, v Wales, had been played there in 1883, with the Ulster club hastily erecting a grandstand to hold 'a large number of people' for the occasion. It blew down in heavy winds just before the next international, v Scotland in January 1884, but was reassembled for the match v England the following month.

A second grandstand was built and the ground hosted major sporting events including athletics meetings. By 1885 the Belfast Corporation had recognized the importance of the venue by extending the city's tram system as far as the entrance, and in an international against Wales in 1887 (Ireland's first ever victory, by 4-1), the crowd in attendance was estimated to be 5,000. In 1888 a 'handsome and commodious' new grandstand replaced the first structure.

From season 1888/89 to 1890/1 Linfield Athletics competed in the Football Association Challenge Cup. On 27th October 1888 Linfield defeated Ulster 7-1 in the second qualifying round at Ulster's ground, in front of 'a fair crowd'. Linfield were then drawn at home to play crack Lancashire side Bolton Wanderers, one of the 12 founder clubs of the English Football League, in the third qualifying round on 17th November 1888. The venue was switched to the Ulster Ground at Ballynafeigh, 'kindly lent for the occasion', presumably to accommodate a larger crowd than was possible at the Linfield Mill. In the event, Bolton sent their reserve, or junior, team to Belfast for the match as their first team had a League game that day, and Linfield won 4-0. 'A very large number of the lovers of genuine football' attended.

In the fourth qualifying round, the two remaining Irish teams in the competition, Linfield and Cliftonville, were drawn together. Following two 3-3 draws, Linfield eventually beat their Belfast rivals 7-0 on 25th December 1888 – the first and only time an FA Cup match was played on Christmas Day. Linfield thus became the first Irish Club to reach the first round proper of the FA Cup. The round consisted of 32 teams, and Linfield were drawn to play away, at Nottingham Forest.

Before the big game, Linfield played a friendly against North End Athletic at the Linfield Mill on Saturday 26th January 1889, winning 7-1. It was to be the last match played by the first team at the Mill, although the Second XI continued to play at the ground for some months. The match against Forest took place in Nottingham - the Linfield team's first trip 'abroad' - on the 2nd February 1889 and finished in a 2-2 draw after extra time was played. The team played a friendly against Bootle en route to Nottingham. The replay against Forest was held on 9th February and the tie was switched to Ballynafeigh. Linfield won the match 3-1.

Estimates of the crowd ranged from between 5,000 and 7,000 spectators. Gate receipts totalled £66 and with admission prices at sixpence and ninepence (for the grandstand, which was 'full for the first time') the paying attendance was probably around 2,500 to 3,500, with ladies entering free of charge along with existing members of the Linfield and Ulster clubs.

It was to be a hollow victory, however, as reported in the local press: 'Having regard to the interest shown in the event, the Ulster ground at Ballynafeigh was fixed upon as the scene of battle, and the crowd of spectators was one of the largest ever seen at a football match in the city. We understand, however, that Linfield scratched in the cup competition to the Forest team, and therefore, the latter will have to meet Chatham. This fact will, we are sure, come as a surprise to many, as it was not by any means generally known in the city on Saturday.'

Various theories were put forward as to why Linfield scratched. One was that, with the winners pre-drawn to play away to Chatham in the south of England, at a ground where spectators did not pay admission, Linfield could ill afford another expensive trip to compete in a tournament they had little chance of winning.

In the days following the game, letters appeared in the Belfast Telegraph with claim and counter claim:

'I was disappointed, when on reading your Saturday's paper, I learned that the match as practically a friendly one. I should be sorry to judge our Linfield friends harshly, and I should be equally sorry to know of such a splendid team being in any way affected by the fact that the public were a little taken in.'

Eventually Linfield provided an explanation:

'Would you kindly allow us space in your valuable paper for a few remarks in reply to "Pro bono publico" which appeared in last evening's edition and to explain to the football public of Belfast the reasons why the Linfield Athletics scratched to Notts Forest in the competition for the English Cup on Saturday last at Ballynafeigh. Your readers are well aware that Linfield travelled to Nottingham on Saturday week to play the Forest Club. One of their backs was unable to cross with the team, and the Committee decided to play Wm. Johnston who had been a member for some time past. According to the English rules a player must have played two matches at least for his club previous to Cup tie date. In Mr Johnston's case this had not been done and some good friend of Irish football had taken great care to inform the Forest Football Club of these facts before arriving in Belfast.

Mr Widdowson, vice-president of the Forest Club, waited on us on Friday evening at 3.30pm... and gave us to five o clock to decide whether we would scratch to Notts Forest and play a friendly match; or whether he would wire Mr Alcock [secretary of the English Football Association] to postpone the Cup tie match until the Mr W. Johnston case was settled. Under these circumstance, the committee of the Linfield Athletic Club decided to scratch to Notts Forest, seeing we would have been thrown out of the Cup competition for our blunder, at the same time agreeing with Mr Widdowson to keep the mater a secret from both teams, for the Linfield team were so determined to beat the Forest team that, had they been told of the arrangement, they would certainly not have played. That, sir, is an explanation of the whole matter. We did what we considered best under the circumstances. If there is any blame to be attached to the Linfield Athletic Club, it does not rest on the team but yours obediently,

John Torrens Financial Sec, Thomas Gordon, Hon. Sec.'

Clearly not short of ambition, Linfield arranged further exhibition matches at Ballynafeigh, against Blackburn Rovers (winners of the FA Cup three years running 1884-1886) and Preston North End (winners of the first Football League 1888-89 and also the FA Cup that year, the first "double", in which they were undefeated, earning the nickname "the invincibles"). Like the previous Cup matches against Blackburn and Notts Forest, these matches were switched to Ballynafeigh to allow for the increasing numbers wishing to attend the games:

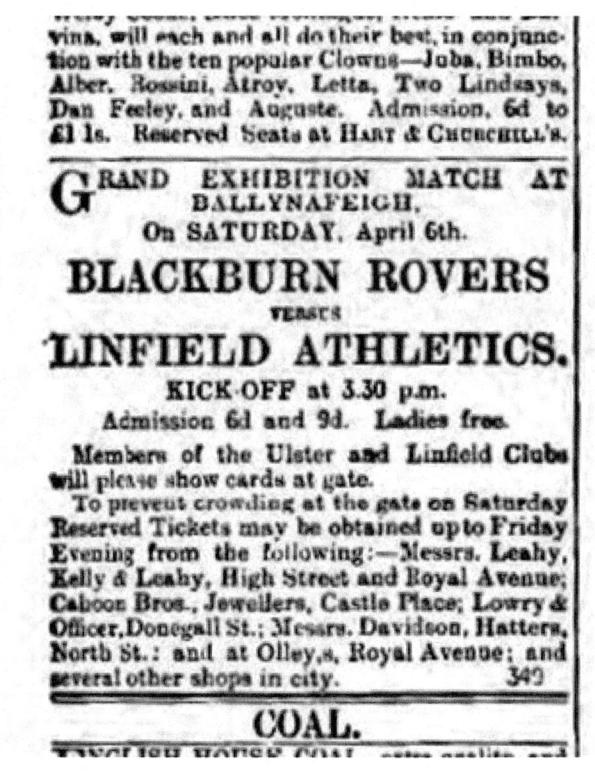

> vina, will each and all do their best, in conjunction with the ten popular Clowns—Juba, Bimbo, Alber, Rossini, Atroy, Letta, Two Lindsays, Dan Feeley, and Auguste. Admission, 6d to £1 1s. Reserved Seats at HART & CHURCHILL'S.
>
> **GRAND EXHIBITION MATCH AT BALLYNAFEIGH,**
> On SATURDAY, April 6th.
> **BLACKBURN ROVERS**
> VERSUS
> **LINFIELD ATHLETICS.**
> KICK-OFF at 3.30 p.m.
> Admission 6d and 9d. Ladies free.
> Members of the Ulster and Linfield Clubs will please show cards at gate.
> To prevent crowding at the gate on Saturday Reserved Tickets may be obtained up to Friday Evening from the following:—Messrs. Leahy, Kelly & Leahy, High Street and Royal Avenue; Caboon Bros., Jewellers, Castle Place; Lowry & Officer, Donegall St.; Messrs. Davidson, Hatters, North St.; and at Olley,s, Royal Avenue; and several other shops in city. 349
>
> **COAL.**

The admission prices – sixpence and nine pence – were on a par with those charged for other "entertainments" in the city, such as in the advert for a music hall entertainment above the one for the match v. Blackburn Rovers. The match ended 3-3 and was played 'in the presence of 3,000 spectators.'

There was an admission price increase to 1 shilling for the next friendly, won by Preston 6-2.

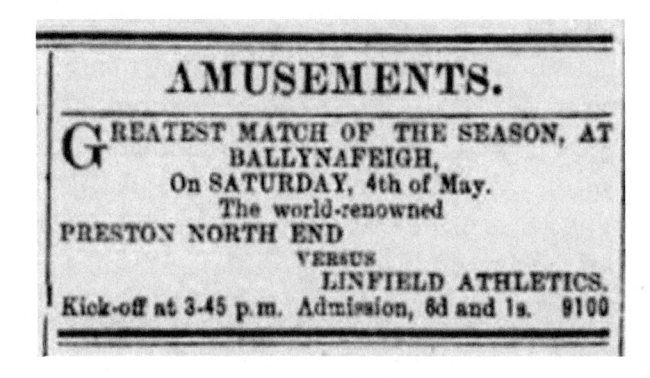

> **AMUSEMENTS.**
> **GREATEST MATCH OF THE SEASON, AT BALLYNAFEIGH,**
> On SATURDAY, 4th of May.
> The world-renowned
> **PRESTON NORTH END**
> VERSUS
> **LINFIELD ATHLETICS.**
> Kick-off at 3-45 p.m. Admission, 6d and 1s. 9100

The Belfast News Letter report of the match was fulsome in its praise of the club: 'The Linfield executive have earned the gratitude of all the followers of the Association code for having brought the visitors to Belfast to show how football is played by a team which is undoubtedly in the foremost rank of football combinations across the water. Having regard to the reputation of the visitors, and to the excellent record of the Linfield team this season, it was not a matter for surprise that there should be a big gate on Saturday. Notwithstanding the very inclement and unfavourable character of the weather, lovers of the game thronged in thousands to Ballynafeigh, and an augmented service of tramcars was largely availed of, with the result that long before the time fixed for the kick-off the assemblage was one of the largest that has ever been seen at a similar exhibition in the city. The splendid stand, which is such a feature in the Ulster ground, was crowded, while there was a solid square all around the field of play, the attendance numbering several thousands.'

Although Linfield were to play more away and neutral matches at Ballynafeigh, the match against Preston was to be their last 'home' one there, as the club had obtained the lease of new premises, at Ulsterville.

The Ballynafeigh grounds were closed in 1902 and all equipment auctioned off after the Ulster club ran into financial difficulties. It was used thereafter for rugby, and briefly for football in 1921 by the Queen's Island club. The grounds are still in existence, known now as the Ulidia playing fields although all traces of the old grandstands and pavilion have disappeared.

3

Ulsterville and homeless

(1889 – 1895)

In 1889 Linfield secured a 10-year lease at £35 per year on land at Ulsterville Avenue, in the south of Belfast about one mile away from the Linfield Mill. The area took its name from Ulsterville House, one of the many grand mansion houses built on the well-drained land in the Malone area for Belfast's emerging merchant class. The site of the ground was initially nothing more than a sand hole, but was within six months converted into an excellent pitch by voluntary labour.

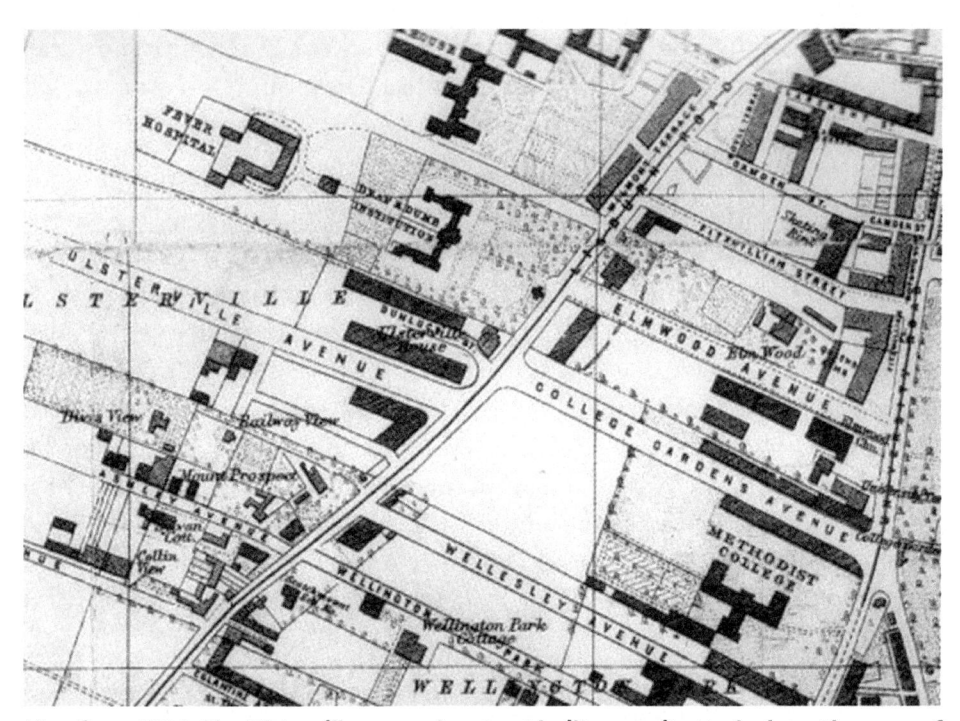

Map from 1884. The Ulsterville ground, not yet built, was situated where the rows of houses in Ulsterville Avenue and Dunluce Street finished

The ground at Ulsterville was situated between present day Ulsterville Avenue and Dunluce Avenue (then known as Dunluce Street). The 1890 Belfast Street Directory records the names and occupations of the residents of the three-storey terraces numbered 3 to 31 on the north side of Ulsterville Avenue, with 'Linfield FC grounds' then listed.

The Ulsterville ground was opened on 7th September 1889 with a friendly match against Distillery. The night before the match, Linfield advertised for new members, who could obtain a season ticket for five shillings. Local newspapers gave a detailed description of the ground:

'[Linfield played Distillery] at Ulsterville, Lisburn Road, to open the splendid new grounds of the Linfield Athletic Club. This plot of land was lately acquired by the committee of the Linfield Club on account of its good locality and central position as it undoubtedly is the most convenient ground in the city: five minutes' walk from the Donegall Pass, along the Lisburn Road, suffices to bring spectators to the field of play, the entrance being by Dunluce Street for the unreserved, and Ulsterville Avenue for the reserved.

The ground has been all re-laid, and is as level as a billiard table. It has been so fixed that it will be quite dry in the wettest weather, being on a sandy subsoil. A magnificent grand stand has been erected on the ground, almost 100 yards long – the longest in Belfast – and will accommodate over a thousand spectators. Terraces have been cut on three sides of the unreserved portion of the ground, and will be found most suitable for the spectators, as a good view of the game will be obtained from them. A magnificent stone-finished pavilion has also been erected. In fact, the ground in every way will be found to be the most comfortable in Belfast.'

'On Saturday afternoon the Linfield Athletics opened their fine new grounds at Ulsterville, Lisburn Road, by a friendly match with Distillery. The match was under the distinguished patronage of the mayor, Mr CC Connor. The evening being unusually fine and the teams both distinguished for their clever exposition of the Association game, there was a very large attendance, the gate being estimated at between five and six thousand. During the past two seasons the Linfield club have shared with Cliftonville the highest degree of public patronage, and as a consequence their old grounds at the Linfield Mill afforded rather slight accommodation. The site of the new ground is a most attractive one, and is within convenient distance from the centre of the city, and easily accessible by tram. The ground has been fitted up regardless of expense on model of the best grounds in England, and every appointment is perfect of its kind.

The property, which has been leased for ten years, is fenced with corrugated iron, and from the reserved and unreserved enclosures separate entrances have been provided, with a view to the convenience of visitors. A neat paling surrounds the playing portion of the grounds, which is thus kept clear without obstructing the view of the spectators. The ground, in addition to being very large, has been levelled and re-laid, under the direction of Mr Butler, of the Balmoral Nurseries, with the result that it now presents a perfectly fine surface. It is also well drained, and will be found desirable for cricket, lacrosse, and other outdoor games.

With a view to the comfort and accommodation of visitors, a magnificent grand stand, extending nearly the entire length of the grounds, has been erected, from which a splendid view of the game can be obtained. In the unreserved portion the ground has been so terraced that every spectator can have a good view of the field.

For the players a handsome pavilion, roofed with corrugated iron, has been erected and fitted with baths and every modern convenience. Indeed, this popular club have spared neither trouble nor expense to make their grounds at once complete and comfortable.'

Linfield Athletics won the opening match against Distillery 3-1, and followed this up with an impressive series of 'home' results:

1889/90

Distillery	07/09/1889	Home	3-1	Friendly
Y.M.C.A.	14/09/1889	Home	5-0	Friendly
Belfast Athletic	21/09/1889	Home	7-0	Friendly
Limavady	05/10/1889	Home	8-1	Friendly
Ulster	12/10/1889	Home	5-1	Friendly
North End Athletic	19/10/1889	Home	10-0	Irish Cup Round 1
Cliftonville	26/10/1889	Home	4-0	FA Cup Round 2
Belfast Athletic	02/11/1889	Home	7-0	Co. Antrim Shield Round 1

Victory over Cliftonville in the FA Cup led to Linfield meeting Distillery in the next round, on 7th December, and in the week before the match 'a splendid stand' was erected for the unreserved portion of visitors. As previewed in the Ulster Football and Cycling News:

'The match will be played at Ulsterville, where the accommodation for spectators is quite stylish, you know! In addition to the reserved stand, capable of seating 1,500 people, the Ulsterville committee have provided a stand for the unreserved to hold 4,000 spectators, so that the facilities for seeing the game on Saturday is of the very best.'

The match was drawn 3-3 in front of a 5,000 crowd, and Distillery won the replay the following week 5-3.

Crowds continued to grow, and an exhibition match against Preston North End on St Patrick's Day, 17th March 1890 attracted 'not less than six thousand spectators'.

Trophy success, however, eluded the club, as they lost to the Gordon Highlanders in the semi-final of the Irish Cup and to the Black Watch in the

Charity Cup. Linfield did reach the final of the County Antrim Shield, but the match, at Ballynafeigh on 22nd March 1890, was marred by violence:

'DISGRACEFUL SCENE OF ROWDYISM.

In connection with Saturday's match at Ballynafeigh, between Linfield and Distillery to decide the holdership of the County Antrim shield, a scene of rowdyism occurred the like of which the Ulster ground - or indeed any ground in Belfast – had never before witnessed. The match, notwithstanding the wet weather, attracted a large crowd, a considerable proportion of which unfortunately belonged to the rough element that has always given the Distillery Club the dubious honour of its support and patronage.

[With Linfield leading 5-3] there remained only about five minutes to play when McIlvenny, who had been twice before cautioned for foul play, offending again in a still more conspicuous manner, was ordered off the field by the referee, Mr. Ellerman. Immediately the ground was invaded by a mob of Distillery partisans belonging to the rough element previously alluded to, and a very disgraceful scene ensued. McKeown, Peden, and other Linfield players who had made themselves particularly obnoxious to the mob, were attacked and struck, and the referee, who had attempted to discharge a difficult duty in a conscientious and fearless manner, was hustled and insulted.

Hundreds of the rough followers of both clubs now swarmed over the field, and various free fights occurred between them, while prominent members of both teams were chaired about by their howling friends. Some blackguards tore down the crossbar of one of the goals and broke it, rendering further play impracticable under any circumstances, even could the ground have been cleared. The arrival of a few policemen stopped the actual fighting, but the roughs still held possession the field, the Distillery players having retired to the pavilion, followed shortly afterwards by the Linfield team. After some consultation among the members of the Committee of the Association it was decided to declare the match off and to withhold the shield.'

LINFIELD ATHLETIC SPORTS
(Under I.A.A.A. and I.C.A. Rules),
At ULSTERVILLE, LISBURN ROAD,
On SATURDAY, 14th June, at 2 p.m.
15 EVENTS, including 100 Yards Championship of Ulster.
Entries Close 3 p.m To-day.
Tickets, 2s 6d (2s if purchased on or before 13th June) and 1s.
Prizes on View, and Entry Forms to be procured, at Messrs. Gibson's, Donegall Place, Belfast, or from
HON. SECS., LINFIELD ATHLETIC SPORTS,
10, Wesley Place, Belfast.

As the press reports on its opening had predicted, the ground at Ulsterville was capable of hosting other sports. 1890 saw the first Linfield sports day, which would become an annual event.

Also in 1890, the club undertook a ballot to raise funds to pay for the grandstand at Ulsterville, with lucrative prizes:

```
LINFIELD ATHLETIC & FOOTBALL CLUB
                BELFAST.

          ~* TO BE BALLOTED FOR, *~
                   IN THE
      LARGE HALL, WORKING MEN'S INSTITUTE,
              QUEEN STREET, BELFAST,
          On FRIDAY, 22nd August, 1890,
In aid of Clearing Off the Debt of the Grand Stand newly erected,
and in aiding to make further Improvements on the New Grounds
at Ulsterville, for the Comfort of the Public, the following Valuable
                      Prizes:—
   1st Prize—Carriage and Pair, New Cottage,
              or Furnish a House complete,
              or Value in Cash,      -    £100
   2nd   „  —Pony and Trap, or a Cook's
              Tourist Excursion Ticket, or
              Value in Cash,    -    -    £50
         AND 28 ADDITIONAL PRIZES.

              SPECIAL PRIZE DRAWING,
For the Benefit of those who Dispose of one or more 10/- Books of
Tickets for the Grand Drawing. A Purchaser of a 10/- Book also
              derives the Benefits of this Drawing.
   1st Prize—Cook's Tourist Excursion Ticket, Value
              in Cash,     -                £20
   and   „  —  Do.     do.      do.    do.   £10
          48 OTHER VALUABLE PRIZES.

            CONSOLATION PRIZE DRAWING.
For the Benefit of Purchasers and Sellers of Books of Tickets value 10/-.
          (This is in addition to the "Special Prize Drawing.")
   1st Prize—Pony and Trap, or Value in Cash,   -   £40
   and   „  —Combination Engine Clock, with Barometer,
              Thermometer, Shade and Stand,    value £20
```

Raising funds for Ulsterville

The following season, 1890-91 saw the creation of the Irish League (the second oldest football league in the world) and Linfield were one of the eight founder member clubs. The team had rapidly progressed to become one of the leading teams in Ireland, and Ulsterville was a ground very few away teams won at. Linfield won the inaugural Irish League, losing only the last of the fourteen games, away to Distillery. The team also won the Irish Cup for the first time, defeating Ulster 4-2 on 14th March 1891 at Solitude, Cliftonville, in front of 5,000 spectators; and the Charity Cup, defeating Ulster 7-1 on 2nd May 1891, again at Solitude.

The ground at Ulsterville was selected by the IFA to host the Ireland v Wales international match on 7th February 1891, Ireland winning 7-2. Prior to then, international and other representative matches were mainly played at Ballynafeigh. In those days, the international team was made up of players drawn exclusively from the Irish League, and six Linfield players were in the Ireland team:

'There was a terrific crush at the entrances and long before three o'clock stands and terraces were crammed to their fullest capacity, those who arrived later having to content themselves with a corner anywhere. There could not have been less than six thousand people present.'

Linfield continued to invite famous clubs from outside Ireland to play exhibition games. Over 6,000 turned out on 27th December 1890 to see Linfield beat a Corinthians team. Other notable visitors to Ulsterville included Partick Thistle (28/02/1891), Wolverhampton Wanderers (09/03/1891), Preston North End (17/03/1891, 'before ten thousand spectators') and Bolton Wanderers (30/03/1891).

Linfield also played a game against a visiting representative team known as the Canadians, winning 3-2 on 29th August 1891. The penalty kick had just been introduced into the Laws of Football, with the idea originating in a proposal from the IFA. During this match the Canadians were awarded a penalty which was duly scored by their right-half Dalton.

This was the first penalty awarded on Irish soil (the first penalty taken occurred in Scotland a few weeks previously, awarded to Royal Albert versus Airdrieonians). Linfield's full back Willie Gordon was the player who gave away the penalty, while his brother Tom Gordon was the goalkeeper who was unable to save it.

In October 1891, the ground was reported as being 'in capital condition, and Linfield intend introducing the goal net (supplied by Messrs. Lowry & Officer) at this match [v Cliftonville].'

In 1891, Ulsterville hosted Lacrosse games, and cricket followed in 1893:

'Linfield's ground, at Ulsterville, was the scene of a rather tame match on Saturday. Enfield made their appearance with an eleven, composed principally of reserve men, and got beaten by six runs. Had time permitted a second innings it is more than possible that the result would have been somewhat different, as Enfield appeared far from home while batting on the bumpy wicket. Sam Torrans [a Linfield Athletic football player] kept wickets very well for Linfield, but he has still to win his spurs at the bat, as one run in each innings doesn't go a long way in making up a score.'

The Linfield football team would go on to win the Irish League and Irish Cup in the 1891/92 and 1892/93 seasons - a treble "double". For the Irish Cup final on 11th March 1893 against Cliftonville, Linfield had "home" advantage:

'It is usual for a cup final to be played on neutral ground, but at the unusual request of both teams Ulsterville was decided on.

The committee anticipating a monster gathering, deemed it advisable to increase the prices of admission from the usual figures to 1 shilling sixpence and 1 shilling. That action had not the desired effect of either increasing their exchequer, or adding to the number of patrons - in fact, many of the greatest enthusiasts and most ardent supporters of the game absented themselves, in order to show their contempt for the course adopted. As the hour for starting approached, a glance round the magnificent grounds of Linfield did not suggest the final for the "Blue Ribbon" of Ireland. Unoccupied seats on the different stands - vacant spaces here and there observable looked somewhat like a decline in the interest that at one time manifested itself, when crowds had to turn away, being unable to penetrate the thick mass of people who thronged to witness the game.'

A few weeks later, on 8th April 1893, the second and final international was played at Ulsterville, Ireland beating Wales 4-3. The IFA had stuck to the same pricing policy used for the Irish Cup final, and the attendance was again lower than expected – estimated at 4,000, and gate receipts of only £50:

'Before dealing with the match we should say that we cannot altogether approve of the action of the Association in raising the admission to a shilling and eighteen pence, but, of course, seeing that they established the precedent in the Irish Cup final, it would scarcely have been consistent to return to the popular prices for an international. The idea of stamping out rowdyism is an admirable one, but why not do this by appointing trustworthy stewards who will do their duty amongst the crowd, and have any unruly individual removed?'

Eviction from Ulsterville

The season 1893-94 was a bad one for Linfield. Star player John Peden was transferred to Newton Heath (later to become Manchester United) and results suffered. The club also had a debt of £1,000 incurred by undertaking work on the ground, and a difficulty with the lease on the ground. It had a clause in it allowing the landlord, a Mr John Ritchie, to repossess the site for house-building should he wish, by giving 6 months' notice. This notice was duly served on 1st May 1893, which in effect meant the club would have to leave by October. Following discussions this was extended until 21st May 1894, allowing Linfield to complete the 1893/94 season.

Linfield took a court case to fight the eviction but the landlord was granted a decree for possession on 16th January 1894. Linfield appealed, but that too was lost.

A further extension to the lease, until 21st September 1894, was granted, allowing Linfield to begin the 1894/95 season at Ulsterville. Linfield began preparing for the reality of an eviction by hosting an event to raise much needed funds on 16th August 1894:

LINFIELD FETE AND CARNIVAL

Yesterday afternoon the fete and bazaar organised in connection with Linfield Athletic and Football Club was opened at the old ground of the club at Ulsterville Avenue. The object of the fete is to clear off debt against the Club, and enable them to start with a clear sheet on their new ground. The club had been compelled by the force of circumstances to seek new ground, which could not be acquired and put in order without money.

The opening ceremony, which took place at four o'clock, was performed by the Lord Mayor. The Chairman, in his opening remarks, drew special attention to the fact that the Linfield was essentially a working men's club, conceived, organised, and maintained by workmen, who, however, had always obtained the goodwill and sympathy of the gentry, merchants, and traders connected with the city.

The Lord Mayor said he had been informed of the history of the Club, and how the grounds on which they now assembled had been acquired in time past and equipped at an expense of a thousand pounds, although the Club, he presumed, was fully aware of the terms upon which they hold the premises, and of the fact that in their case no Act of Parliament could be passed to compensate evicted tenants. (Laughter.) They were now compelled to seek fresh ground, and in order to do so sought to replenish their war chest. This was a laudable desire'.

The landlord agreed a stay of execution until 27th December by payment of an increase in rent, allowing the team to commence the 1894/95 season still playing at Ulsterville, but when a further substantial rise was imposed, Linfield refused to pay. The last Linfield match at Ulsterville was on 15th December 1894, against Cliftonville.

In January 1895, the Athletic News reported that 'the club have secured a new ground on Strandmillis Road, not far from their old one, and quite as central, which will be ready next season. I trust nothing will go against them, as we could ill afford to lose such a strong club.'

Linfield received their marching orders to leave Ulsterville on 12th January 1895. The tone of a Belfast New Letter's report of the eviction was quite benign:

'Several matches were down for settlement on Saturday, but the weather interfered, and none of them came off. The most important of these was the inter-city match between Derry and Belfast, which was to have been played at Ulsterville. Before, however, the weather interfered to stop the match, the landlord placed an effective bar in the way by putting in a bailiff under an ejectment decree granted some twelve months ago. The Linfield Club are not indebted to Mr John Ritchie, the landlord, for any rent, and the decree obtained is simply one for possession of the ground.'

However the report carried in the Manchester Courier and Lancashire General advertiser suggests the ground was taken with some force:

'The grounds of the crack Irish football team, the Linfield Athletic, at Ulsterville, Belfast, were on Saturday seized by the sub-sheriff under a decree obtained for possession by the landlord. The affair, which has caused a great sensation in Irish football circles, was kept a profound secret until Saturday morning, when the sheriff's officers, accompanied by a considerable force of police, seized the place.'

Homeless (Jan 1895 – Sept 1896)

Whatever the ins and outs of the eviction, Linfield were now homeless, the potential for a move to a ground at Strandmillis having fallen through for reasons unknown. Cliftonville immediately offered Linfield the use of their ground for 'play and training' but the rest of the season was played at opponents' grounds or at neutral venues. Even with this handicap, Linfield's name was inscribed on several of the trophies, including the Irish Cup, clinched with a 10-1 victory against Dublin-based Bohemians at Solitude on 23rd March 1895.

On 11th May 1895, "Ulsterville Rangers" – Linfield in all but name – played a friendly at Solitude against "Solitude Nomads" to raise funds for a new ground for Linfield.

The club continued to search for a new ground, with the following reported in August 1895:

'Speaking of Linfield's want of a ground, they are, according to the latest advices, looking after Belview ground at Ravenhill Road, Belfast. They may get it, but it seems to me a case of the drowning man clutching at a straw in Linfield's case, as they are in desperate straits to get rest for the sole of their feet. The ground referred to is a poor one, and at the very end of a tram line, and a considerable distance from the city. At the same time let Linfield get a ground or not, as they are the champion club they are deserving of every sympathy in their present predicament.'

Later that month it seemed that Linfield might return to Ulsterville, as the Scottish Referee reported:

"I am pleased to hear that Linfield have secured their old ground, from which they were so unceremoniously bundled out last January, and which did the landlord no good, as judged by his coming to terms again.'

However, this possible return fell through and in September 1895 it was reported that a site at Balmoral had been secured:

'Linfield, so far, have not got ground, but it is freely stated a plot at Balmoral has been settled, for which the agreement is about to be signed. Undoubtedly, if this is the case, no one will begrudge the champions rest for "the soles of their feet," as the other clubs do not seem as if they mean to have any sentiment over the allowing of the club to play on their ground, when Linfield have choice of ground. I believe Cliftonville are charging them a fixed sum for the use of Solitude tomorrow, which Linfield are forced to pay, and this shows how the wind blows.'

'The only regrettable feature now in connection with the play is the absence of Ulsterville. As the game now stands, it is a matter of extreme importance that each team should be on its best legs, and Linfield are undoubtedly handicapped very heavily through being, as it were, without house or home. It is suggested that the Blues may soon be comfortably settled down in the Balmoral district, and we are very pleased there is even a prospect of this, but they can never hope to find any quarters to suit them so well as the famous Ulsterville enclosure.'

The Athletic News was optimistically reporting in August 1895 that 'Linfield's new ground at Balmoral is an accomplished fact, and they are busy putting it in shape.' However, Linfield would eventually play all of the 1895-96 season without a home ground, with 'home' games played at the grounds of opponents, Linfield invariably having to pay a rental charge to the home club, but sharing the gate receipts equally.

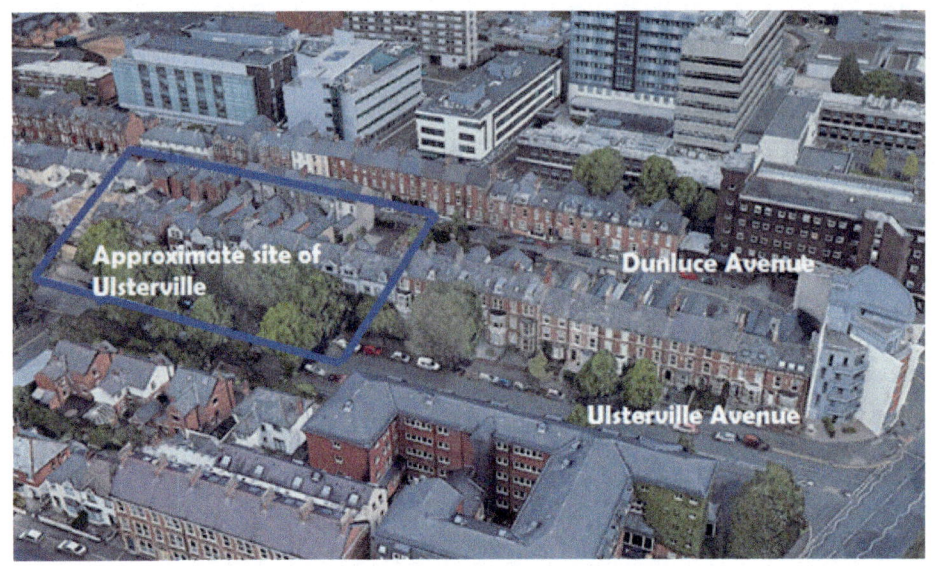

A modern day aerial photo of Ulsterville Avenue and Dunluce Avenue, with the approximate location of the Ulsterville ground shown in Blue

4

Balmoral ground, Myrtlefield

(1896 – 1905)

The new ground was in the Balmoral area of south Belfast – one of a number of such areas named after royal residences, others including Windsor and Osborne. Although Balmoral is now a well-populated and desirable residential area, in the 1890's it was quite rural to the north and west, with the residences on the other side of the Lisburn Road consisting of detached houses for the 'well-to-do' middle classes. Just south of the ground was a home for cats and dogs. The distance from the traditional Linfield heartland of Sandy Row and around Ulsterville was over three miles and was initially considered a handicap for supporters wishing to attend games.

The Balmoral ground at Myrtlefield Park is clearly shown on the top centre of this map as "football ground". The ground was sited roughly where the current Lislea Drive is, just off the Lisburn Road and close to the Balmoral railway station, bottom left

The grounds were not well developed on their opening on 5th September 1896, in an Irish League game against the 2nd North Stafford Regiment, Linfield losing by six goals to one. There was no pavilion yet, and a local hostelry was used by the teams for changing. The markings of the pitch were only completed 10 minutes before the kick-off.

The Belfast News Letter report of the next match, against Cliftonville the following week, was not complimentary about the new facilities:

29

'Cliftonville visited Linfield at their new ground, Balmoral, and after a most interesting match, returned home winners by four goals to three. We fear that it will be a long time before the new Linfield ground becomes as popular as was Ulsterville. At present it is in a very incomplete state. There is a great need for a railing along the unreserved side of the field, as on Saturday the spectators encroached on the field of play on several occasions, despite the efforts of a number of the officials of the club.'

A few months later, at least some improvements had been made. A pavilion was erected behind one of the goals, and a separate dressing room erected for the referee. However, it was clear that the new ground was not yet on a par with the grounds of other clubs, as the Belfast Weekly News pointed out in December 1896: 'We understand Linfield intend playing their fixture with Cliftonville next Saturday at Solitude, and not at Balmoral, as previously arranged. We think this is a wise decision on the part of the Linfield executive, their ground at present is quite unfit for first-class football.'

Further ground improvements were made in following seasons and, in November 1897 in a move that would have made it easier to get to and from the ground, the Great Northern Railway proposed to establish a station or platform at Myrtlefield for the convenience of spectators. There are, however, no records of the station ever being built – perhaps not surprising as the existing Balmoral station, shown on the map above, was long established, having opened in 1858. Perhaps it was intended to be competition for the trams, as the Dublin-based newspaper Sport had reported earlier that year that the 'Linfield ground has the name of being out of the way, which is opposite to the fact, as it is very easy of access. The tramway passes the ground ... The ground can be reached in about 20 minutes, the only other ground beating it in point of easy access being Grosvenor Park' [home of Distillery].

In 1898 the ground underwent a complete system of drainage, and the pavilion was improved by the laying on of water and baths. Linfield also decided to bank the unreserved side of their ground, and to enable them to carry out the improvement they arranged to lease the field adjacent to the ground. By November that year, the Belfast Evening Telegraph reported that the ground was being 'terraced to the height of twenty feet.'

As had been the case at Ulsterville, the ground was used for other purposes during the summer months, and the Rugby Lacrosse Club was accommodated to play there in the summer of 1899.

A grandstand, described as 'not of a very formidable sort', was erected behind one of the goals and was the scene of a near disaster at the 0-0 match against Distillery on 7th October 1899, attended by an estimated

4,000 spectators. There were around 500 people packed in the stand when, just after half-time, it gave way with an almighty crash. A number of people were injured, among them Fred Jordan, winner of the 50 and 100 mile Irish Road Club Cycling Championship, who had three ribs fractured. About half-a-dozen persons were conveyed in ambulances to Belfast Royal Hospital. A number of bicycles, which had been placed underneath the stand, were badly damaged. As the Irish News reported, 'Linfield have not had much luck at this enclosure, which since they took possession in the matter of repairs has cost them a pretty penny.'

The Balmoral ground was rarely chosen for neutral or representative games. No Ireland internationals were played there (although Ireland did play England at the nearby Balmoral Showgrounds, owned by the North-East Agricultural Association, in 1902). The negative comments expressed by the Irish News and Belfast Morning News in April 1901 help explain:

'Though the County Antrim Association were enabled, in spite of the terrible weather during last week, to bring off their Shield final on Saturday [between Cliftonville and Glentoran], the result, from a financial point of view, can hardly be viewed by them with satisfaction. To begin with, the venue of the match was a mistake, and how the Association passed over Grosvenor Park for Linfield's enclosure is hard to say. At the time the ground was settled a large majority, I understand, plumped for playing it at Balmoral, but in doing so I hardly think the interests of the Association were in any way furthered. However, it is over and done with, but I fancy even though it seems to have been case of pandering sentiment, no more finals will be decided at Balmoral.'

Despite, or perhaps because of the low regard in which the ground was held, plans were announced in August 1901 for the construction of a grandstand to run the whole length of the reserved side, with accommodation for several thousand spectators.

At least on the pitch the Linfield team continued to win trophies, with the Irish league and Cup "double" being achieved in 1897/98, 1901/02, and 1903/04. Crowds were generally good – a game against Distillery on 20th October 1900 attracted an estimated crowd of 7,000, paying a gate of £126. The opening home Irish League game on 31st August 1904, again against Distillery, had a reported crowd of 8,000.

However despite the team's success and the healthy attendances, the overall unsuitability of the Balmoral ground, its distance from Linfield's traditional supporter base and the fact of the ground being rented from a landlord – an arrangement much in the minds of the Linfield Committee following the Ulsterville eviction – encouraged the Club to continue the search for new premises.

It's likely the fact that the four big rival clubs of Linfield in Belfast were already established in their permanent homes also added to Linfield's desire for their own home. Distillery had opened their ground at Grosvenor Park in 1889 and remained there on and off until forced to abandon the ground at the height of civil unrest in the early 1970's; Cliftonville's ground in the north of the city, Solitude (and still their home to the present day) had opened in 1890. The Belfast Celtic club, formed as a junior club in 1891 and competing as a senior club in the Irish League from the 1896/97 season, had opened their ground, Celtic Park, in 1901, and Glentoran, based in the east of the city, settled in their permanent (and still current) home, The Oval, in 1903. Thus it was that the Linfield Committee came to secure a patch of land that would eventually become the site of the Club's permanent home, at Windsor Park.

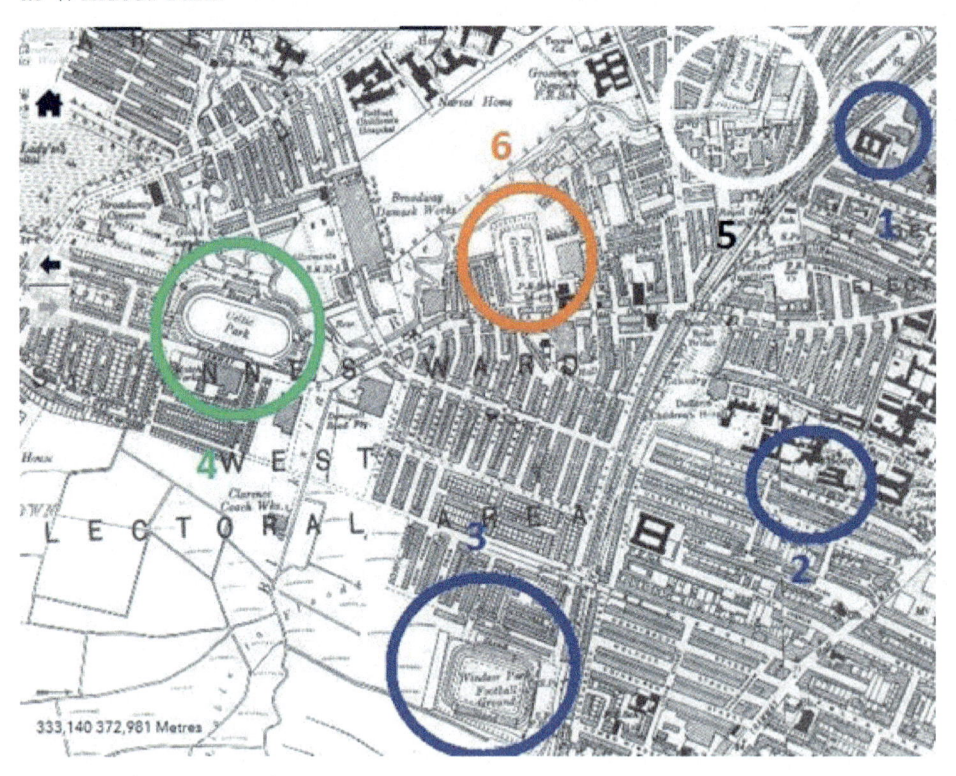

Map showing the locations of grounds:
1 Linfield Mill (approximate)
2 Ulsterville (approximate)
3 Windsor Park
4 Celtic Park, Belfast Celtic
5 Grosvenor Park, Distillery
6 Broadway United

5

Windsor Park

Purchase and Development 1904 – 1910

Belfast city in 1904 was continuing to expand, and the granting of city status in 1888 prompted the Belfast Corporation to commission the building of a City Hall. Construction began in 1898 and would be completed in 1906. Elsewhere in the city centre the imposing Church House, home to the General Assembly of the Presbyterian Church in Ireland, would open in 1905.

It was in this Edwardian era of expansion and prosperity that Windsor Park was born. Its development in many ways matched the building of football grounds across the United Kingdom, often similarly created on formerly derelict land unsuitable for other uses. In the period 1905 – 1920, some 58 of the 92 English league clubs established their original grounds.

In 1904, Arthur McDermott, Linfield committee member, had learned on the grapevine that a large piece of the Bog Meadows was scheduled to come on the market and it seemed a suitable site on which to build a new stadium. On 1st August 1904, he conducted the Linfield Committee on an inspection tour, and met the landowner Rev R. J. Clarke, who agreed to sell immediately. The Committee's reaction was instant; they didn't want him to change his mind and, within a few days a legal agreement had been drawn up and signed with the final completion on October 1, 1904. David W. Foy, Linfield treasurer, was the Linfield signatory to the document.

The Bog Meadows was a large, marshy area of land in south Belfast which acted as a flood plain. A letter of the time to the Belfast News Letter commented on its dubious attractions:

'I was pleased to see in your issue today a letter on the subject of the open sewers in the Bog Meadows, and, having been over this ground recently, I can corroborate every statement made by your correspondent. One has to see these filthy drains and feel the horrible, sickening stench they emit before realising the true condition of affairs in this neighbourhood. When a heavy rainfall occurs, as is well known, these meadows become flooded, and the sewage from the drains is spread over the surrounding grass land, where dairy cattle are grazed during the greater part of the year. Your correspondent is not far wrong, I fancy, in heading his letter "Typhoid Made Easy" and I hope that the members of the City Council for the Windsor and other wards interested will take this matter in hands and be able to move the Public Health Department to take action without delay'.

Once the land was purchased, Linfield moved quickly to prepare it for use. An advert seeking tenders for the construction was placed in the local newspapers in October 1904, and hopes were high that the ground would be ready for Linfield to enter into possession on Easter Monday 1905. The venture was not without cost, and in November 1904 Linfield established a Committee with the task of raising £500 to complete the new ground, which it was announced was to be known as Windsor Park.

CONTRACTS.

LINFIELD FOOTBALL AND ATHLETIC CLUB.

THE Committee of above Club invite TENDERS at once for the Enclosing of their New Grounds at Lower Windsor, in accordance with Plans and Specification to be seen at 123 Albion Place, Dublin Road.
1460   S. CLOSE, Secretary.

Tender for construction of the new ground, October 1904

By December, the ground had been completely walled in; by January 1905, the ground was taking shape. Ralph the Rover, football correspondent for the Belfast Telegraph reported:

'I have paid another visit to the new around at Windsor for the Linfield Club, and must say I was agreeably surprised at the immense progress made since my last visit. The ground has now been completely levelled, relaid, and walled in and unless one saw it they would have no idea of the great size of the enclosure. The banking on the unreserved side of the ground is now being proceeded with with all possible expedition'.

The land was bound at its south eastern side by the main railway line from Belfast to Dublin, first opened in 1839 and operated by the Great Northern Railway (Ireland) Company, (GNR). Otherwise, the ground was surrounded by a marshy wasteland – housing and industrial development would come much later.

The Linfield team continued to play at the Balmoral ground in the early part of 1905 whilst the new ground was being prepared. In March 1905, however, the Balmoral ground was made available by its landlord "to let". Ralph the Rover again:

'The place that knew the Linfield club so long will know it now no more for ever. In other words, Balmoral ground is to let. Had there only been a little give and take on the part of the owners the Linfield club might have established themselves permanently at Balmoral but in another month they will have transferred themselves bag and baggage to their new ground at Windsor, which is rapidly nearing completion'.

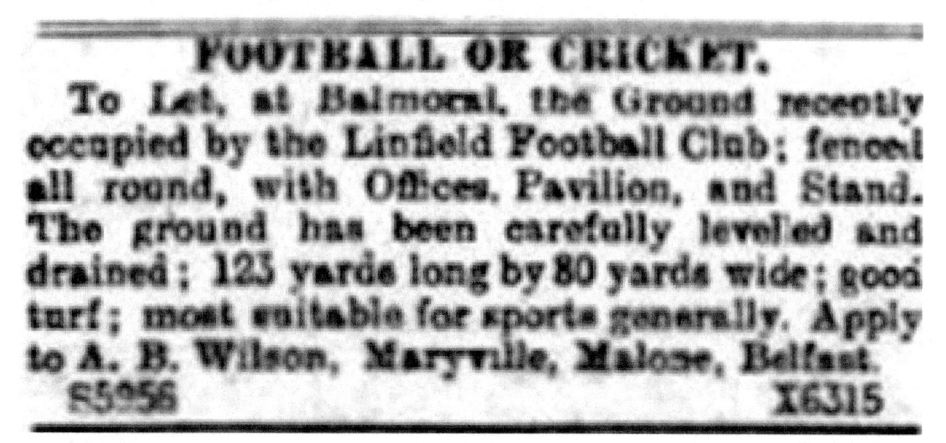

> **FOOTBALL OR CRICKET.**
> To Let, at Balmoral, the Ground recently occupied by the Linfield Football Club; fenced all round, with Offices, Pavilion, and Stand. The ground has been carefully levelled and drained; 125 yards long by 80 yards wide; good turf; most suitable for sports generally. Apply to A. B. Wilson, Maryville, Malone, Belfast.
> 55956   X6315

The Balmoral ground is advertised as available To Let, April 1905

By May 1905 the ground was in Linfield's possession, and the ground at Balmoral taken over by the Stranmillis Cricket and Tennis Club:

> **STRANMILLIS CRICKET AND LAWN TENNIS CLUB.**
> The annual meeting of this club has just been held. There was a large attendance of members. The reports were received and adopted, and office-bearers appointed for coming season. It was announced that the grounds lately occupied by Linfield F.C. at Balmoral had been secured. It is intended to relay the grounds, and when this is done the club hope to have a first-class cricket pitch, which should meet a demand long felt in the district. There has been a large turnout of members at the nets during the past week, which augurs well for the future of the club.

The grand opening

Following a trial match on 19th August, the grand opening match, a friendly against Distillery, was scheduled for Saturday 26th August 1905. However, it had to be postponed, as the Belfast News Letter reported: 'A deluge of rain robbed Linfield, the famous Blues, of what would have been a bumping gate, and this is the more to be regretted from the fact that the occasion was the opening of their new ground at Windsor Park'. The opening match was re-arranged for the following Tuesday, and the Londonderry Sentinel described the event: 'Linfield brought off their postponed game with Distillery on Tuesday. The grounds looked exceedingly well and reflect great credit on the enterprise of the Linfield Executive. The turf was in fine order, notwithstanding the fact that the lower portion of the ground was under water on Saturday last owing to the floods. There was no scoring.'

The advert for the aborted opening match, August 1905

The first official, Irish League, match was played on Saturday September 2nd 1905 against Glentoran, with Linfield winning 1-0. The recorded gate receipts were £112, considerably more than at other games that day – a reflection perhaps of curiosity, and the large support both clubs enjoyed. The admission prices were six pence and nine pence (the same admission price as matches at The Mill some 17 years previously). These admission prices and gate receipts would indicate a paying crowd in the region of 3,500 – 4,500, most likely swelled by Linfield members and season ticket holders – paid for by annual subscription and entitling admission to all home matches. Demand for these Linfield members' and season tickets was reported as 'unparalleled in the history of the club'.

An Irish News and Belfast Morning News report of a match later that month against Belfast Celtic gave a glowing report on the new ground: 'A burning summer sun heralded the Celts' first visit to the new home of the Blues, Windsor Park, an enclosure which certainly reflects the greatest credit on the enterprise of the management. Windsor Park has one great advantage over their former enclosure at Balmoral - viz, a reasonable distance from the centre of the city, and can be approached from any direction. This latter to the Celts' followers at Balmoral would have been a boon, but I am glad to say that, as in political methods, a great change has made its appearance in the people. On Saturday the best of good feeling prevailed, and every person in the ground could encourage his favourites in a legitimate manner. This is as it should be, and will do much to popularise the game in the ground. The turf was in fair order, much resembling the Celtic Park pitch, an uneven surface being noticeable in places. There is plenty of space for spectators, the latter being kept a good distance from the players, thereby giving visitors freedom in their movements, out of earshot of remarks which often spoil games by an ebullition of bad feeling amongst the performers'.

The ground was likely quite basic upon its opening. There was initially no seated or covered accommodation, and the sloped banking spectators stood on would have been made up of rubble, muck and cinders. Any "terrace" would have been constructed from planks of wood, or railway sleepers, laid on top of the rough ground. The ground did have a pavilion, erected at the end nearest the railway by club member, David Johnston, who had been responsible for work at the old Ulsterville ground.

It's also likely that there were initially two separate standing enclosures for spectators – a reserved and an unreserved - as two different admission prices were charged for the opening game. As with other football grounds, the "reserved" area on the south side would have been favoured as the sun would have been behind the spectators and hence not shining in their eyes. In November 1905 Linfield laid seven new drains with the intent of making the playing pitch one of the driest in the city.

Access to the new grounds was mainly from the Lisburn Road and Lower Windsor Avenue, and spectators had to use a level crossing to get across the GNR rail lines. Access was enhanced by the electrification of the Belfast Corporation Tramway network in 1905, with trams running from the city centre along the Lisburn Road. This was welcomed by the Northern Whig newspaper in December 1905:

'The electric tram service on the Lisburn Road greatly facilitated matters, and when the revised fares come into operation the Linfield enclosure will receive a still greater share of patronage. It is pity that it is on the other side of the railway. Perhaps after a time it may be possible to erect an overhead footbridge. In the meantime the Linfield Executive might busy themselves improving the approaches to the ground. On a wet day I tremble to think of the objurgations which would descend upon their devoted heads from mud-bespattered enthusiasts'.

Later that month, and in anticipation of a large Christmas holiday crowd, the Whig commented:

'No match this season has created such an amount of excitement as the meeting of Distillery and Linfield on Christmas morning at Windsor Park, and extra arrangements have been made there for the accommodation of a record attendance. The teams at present are at the top of the League Championship table, and, as the team which is fortunate in securing the points in this game will in all probability be entitled to the title of champions, it is only to be expected that the Executive and players of both Clubs are making strenuous efforts to pull off a victory. In anticipation of a great crowd the entrances at the ground have been doubled, and it is hoped that intending spectators will assist the Executive by falling into line at gates so as to avoid unnecessary crushing. A special tram service has been arranged for, and trains will also run to Windsor at convenient intervals, so that the holding capacity of the Blues' new home should be thoroughly tested on this occasion'.

In 1906, the area around the pitch was fenced. Crowds were sizable; an Irish Cup match against Distillery on Saturday 3rd November 1906 attracted a reported crowd of 7,000. The team was successful on the pitch too, winning the Irish League in the 1906-07 season, and repeating the feat in the following two seasons.

Building of a seated grand stand

In 1907, Sam Close, the Linfield Club secretary, oversaw the construction of a seated grandstand on the south side. In January, Ralph the Rover wrote: 'I am informed that the Linfield Club propose erecting a covered stand the whole length of the reserved enclosure at Windsor Park. Its erection will begin immediately after the close of the present season, and be continued right through the summer months until it has been completed. A grandstand at Windsor will be an inestimable boon to those who are in the habit of frequenting the ground. I am glad to see that Linfield have at last decided to move in this matter. The appearance and comfort of the ground will be increased twofold by the erection of such a stand'.

Work on the new grandstand continued throughout 1907. In April it was reported that Linfield had already asked for quotations for the erection of their new grandstand. By September the Irish News reported that construction was ready to go: 'The plans for the new grandstand at Windsor Park are now in the hands of Corporation officials, and it is expected that official sanction will be given during the present week, when the erection will at once be proceeded with. The contract, which closely touches four figures, has been given to the same contractors who erected the [Belfast] Celtic stand roofing. It will be 120 yards long, enclosing ten tiers of seats'.

When constructed, the stand did not quite run the full length of the pitch. In front of the new stand's rows of seating was a standing enclosure. The cover was of the type known as a "Belfast" roof, and similar covers were present or would be built at Celtic Park, Grosvenor Park, Solitude and The Oval. The Belfast Roof - or more accurately the Belfast roof truss - had been developed by Belfast's linen industry and were commonly used for large sheds, warehouses and barns, and had the advantage of being lightweight yet robust.

A composite still picture taken from a 1927 newsreel showing the original 1907 grand stand

However, there were some teething problems with the ground and the new grand stand as evidenced in various newspaper reports in 1908: 'Both the Cliftonville and Linfield grounds have, I hear, undergone rough usage at the hands of the storm, the railings at part of the first-named enclosure having suffered badly, while the Windsor enclosure has also suffered its own share of damage. Both will be put into ship-shape at once'.

Ralph the Rover called attention to the bad state of the road at the White Swan Laundry, which was described as in an almost impassable state for those living in Donegall Road and Sandy Row:

'A few loads of cinders along the footpaths would do an immense good, and save wading through a sea of mud. The Windsor sward, on which I cast my critical eye, pleased me muchly. It looked as clean and trim as a freshly laid bowling green. But while I congratulate the Linfield Executive, might I suggest that the accommodation for the spectators might be further improved? On a blustery day the wind that whistles through the covered stand is most uncomfortable. This fine erection should be extended as soon as possible and closed in at both ends.'

There were also calls from spectators for a covered unreserved area.

Further improvements

Development and expansion of the ground continued apace. In September 1908, more improvements were reported:

'Linfield Club are making extensive improvements for the accommodation of large crowds. Both reserved and unreserved sides are being banked up, some hundreds of loads of filling-in material being deposited during the past few weeks. On the unreserved side, in addition, twelve tiers of terracing have been erected, which, when finished, will accommodate a vast crowd. The club need now have only one anxiety – that is, the crowd to use the accommodation provided'.

'Saturday's crush on the grandstand at Windsor demonstrated the absolute necessity for an entrance to the Press-Box other than by the crowded steps in front, and I am glad to learn, and so will all members of the "Fourth Estate", that the Linfield club propose erecting a means of ingress and egress from the rear of the reserved stand'.

The banking behind one goal, at the Bog Meadows, or "mountain" end – reflecting its relatively close proximity to Belfast's Divis mountain – assumed the name Spion Kop, the colloquial name for a number of similar single tier terraces at football grounds in the United Kingdom, and named for the resemblance to a hill near Ladysmith, South Africa, that was the scene of the Battle of Spion Kop in January 1900 during the Second Boer War.

The most famous such area was created at Anfield, home of Liverpool FC, in 1906. The term was used in connection with Windsor Park in early 1909, with the Belfast Telegraph recording: 'Arrangements had been made at Windsor to accommodate a record crowd, and a record crowd would have faced the slopes of Spion Kop had the weather not broken on Friday last with such disastrous effects'.

First Irish Cup final at Windsor Park, and the "Blue Carnival"

Windsor Park hosted its first Irish Cup final on 3rd April 1909 when Cliftonville and Bohemians played out a 0-0 draw. Later that year, on the evening of the 30th June, 'glorious weather again favoured the "Blue Carnival" promoted by the Linfield Football and Athletic Club on the well-known grounds of the organisation at Windsor Avenue, with the object of raising £1,000 to provide the ground with additional covered stands.'

Such methods of fund-raising were quite common with most of the prominent clubs organising raffles, lotteries and bazaars.

The fund-raising was a success, with £100 left over after the expenses and the contract price were settled and in September 1909 Linfield embarked on further improvements:

'Today the Linfield people enter upon the erection of a covering over the unreserved portion of Windsor Park, and hope by the first of December to see this much required improvement a reality. Quite half of the enclosure will be covered in. Linfield have in view the English international, and all efforts are to be concentrated towards securing the greatest match of the year.'

'The contract for the erection of the new covered enclosure on the unreserved [north] side of Windsor Park was signed on Saturday evening, and work will be commenced on this day week. The covering will be 60 feet longer than the reserved stand, making a total of 180 feet in all. For months past the ground has been in process of filling up, and the banked earth has now been terraced'.

By November 1909, the new cover was almost ready, as was a new press box, most likely sited at the railway end of the ground, next to the pavilion: 'The Linfield Press box will be completely overhauled and renovated by Saturday next. Habituees of the ground will not know it, and a surprise is in store for those pressmen who have been in the habit of paying periodical visits to Windsor Park. It is to be encased entirely with glass and made much more comfortable in every way than it was. The new unreserved covered stand will be taken over from the contractor on Saturday next also.'

The improvements had increased the capacity of the ground to the largest in Ireland. Ralph the Rover was given an exclusive preview:

'At the special request of the Linfield Club I made a special visit to Windsor Park last Friday. I was immediately handed a plan of the ground and the following certificate of its holding capacity, prepared by that eminent firm of architects and civil engineers, Messrs Young and McKenzie:

Unreserved enclosure	42,556
Unreserved covered	5,270
Reserved covered	3,000
Total	50,826

Eighteen inches has been allotted to each spectator, and yet I am assured that ample room still remains. It is the intention of the club to erect a new two-story pavilion in the reserved corner of the ground on similar lines to the one at Solitude, while it is also contemplated at an early date to proceed with the erection of an addition to the present grand stand'.

The new cover was formally opened at the match between Linfield and Belfast Celtic on Saturday 27th November 1909, Linfield winning 2-0. This new cover was, like that of the seated grand stand on the south side, constructed using a "Belfast" roof truss and was erected at the unreserved north side of the ground. It would remain there, in extended form, until 1982.

Crowds continued to grow: the final of the 1909 Steel and Sons Cup tournament for junior clubs was held at Windsor Park on Christmas Day

Composite photo from newsreel of the cover over the unreserved terrace, 1924

between Larne and Oldpark Corinthians and was attended by 16,000 spectators.

First international match at Windsor Park

In November 1909 Linfield were awarded the hosting of an international match, played as part of the annual British Home Championship. It was versus Scotland, the tie against England game being awarded to Solitude, home of Cliftonville FC, a month earlier. The decision was taken by vote at the monthly meeting of the IFA, at which the Leinster Association made a bid for the England match to be played in Dublin. The proceedings were reported by the Irish News and Belfast Morning News:

'The motion to play the match in Dublin was lost by 16 votes to 6, and a motion was subsequently carried to play it Belfast. Cliftonville and Windsor Park were nominated grounds for the English match. Mr Warwick said that Windsor Park would accommodate 50,000 people. Cliftonville's ground was selected by 10 votes to 6. Regarding the Scotch match, Dublin was moved as the venue, but Mr Fitzsimmons said that the match did not now appeal to the Dublin people. Windsor Park and Grosvenor Park were, therefore, proposed, the former being selected by 17 votes to 2'.

However not everyone was happy with the behaviour of the home spectators at club matches, as Ralph the Rover noted: 'Fred McKee has complained to me again about the treatment meted out to him by the spectators behind the mountain goal at Windsor on Monday last. If you don't do something to put a stop to this ungentlemanly behaviour, Linfield, your enclosure will soon get a bad name amongst visiting teams.'

Linfield pressed ahead with more improvements before the big Ireland versus Scotland international match played on the 19th March 1910:

'The terracing of the Linfield enclosure has been proceeding apace for weeks past, and full to the brim it will present a goodly sight. More turnstiles, I am afraid, and more expedition in their manipulation will be necessary to get the crowd in in reasonable time. But the Association, and the Linfield Club, may be well left to deal with all these exigencies.'

Advice on the best way to get to the ground was given to supporters in advance by the Northern Whig:

'All roads should lead to Windsor Park next Saturday, but unfortunately there are only two that really do, and here is a problem that will tax the organising capabilities of the IFA. Linfield is at present a most inaccessible ground. This is not the fault of the Club, as they could not find suitable acreage on this side of the railway line. It is the railway line that is the trouble. It cuts off the ground from its natural outlets to the Lisburn Road, and so huge crowds must be manipulated in the narrow space of a level crossing. There may be little difficulty getting the crowd into the ground, as they will be coming continuously for a couple of hours. But when the game is over and there is a rush for the trams I tremble to think of that crossing. Methinks there will be danger on the line. I am sure the IFA are alive to their responsibilities on this matter, but the sooner they take the public into their confidence the better will be the gate.

There is another route leading to the Linfield enclosure which avoids the railway line altogether. It is bit circuitous, but it will be quite safe, and should be taken by all residents coming from Sandy Row, Grosvenor Road, and Falls Road districts, as it will make very little difference to them, and thus relieve the congestion at Windsor Avenue. Cars and other vehicles might also find this route easier to negotiate.

I have no personal knowledge of the road, but here it is as it was described to me by a man who uses it regularly. You go up the Donegall Road as far as the railway bridge, and then turn down Donegall Avenue, which brings you alongside the grounds. It may be a little extra walk, but that would not be a great inconvenience compared with a crush and a panic, as might easily happen on the Windsor Park side. This alternative method of reaching the match might be advertised widely, as it is only known to residents of the district. When we get the trams on the Donegall Road and overhead bridges on the railway we shall be able to go to and come from Windsor in peace and comfort. In the meantime, with the thousands of people who will be patronising the ground for the first time, too many precautions cannot be taken.'

Ireland won the match 1-0, the first victory over Scotland on home soil. The match was well attended: 'The attendance must have reached a total of almost 25,000 people, and there was ample accommodation for more. The enclosure has undergone a complete transformation, and now is perhaps the most commodious ground in Ireland.'

Linfield were praised for their management of the match, and solutions were being proposed for the access problems, as Ralph the Rover wrote:

'Preparations, I am given to understand, are already in progress for the erection of the three new bridges over the railway lines at Windsor, and these will probably be complete and ready for use before nest season comes round. I was at Windsor on Thursday last, and saw the engineers taking the dimensions for the new structures, which will be a means of greater safety and convenience to the patrons of the Linfield club, and obviate the present annoying delays at the gates over the railway. Never in the history of international matches were the arrangements so perfect, and so satisfactorily carried out.' The Northern Whig, too, was fulsome in its praise:

'May I congratulate the Linfield Club particularly and the IFA generally on the remarkable improvement in Windsor Park. It was a wonderful piece of work performed unostentatiously in a short space of time. Honour to whom honour is due, when I find out who the "workers" were I shall see they get due recognition from me. It is safe to say that Windsor Park will be the scene of many another international, and I trust many another Irish victory. Curiously enough, the first international ever played at a Linfield ground - old Ulsterville - resulted in a victory over Wales. Lucky Linfield. Lucky for themselves and lucky for Ireland. May their shadows never grow less'.

The IFA's main source of income came from the hosting of Irish Cup semi-finals and finals, and the one or two international games each season. It would have been in the IFA's interests to maximise revenue by hosting the most popular games at the largest stadium, and, insofar as contemporary records show, Windsor Park fitted the bill.

The sole Home International in 1911, versus Wales, was awarded to Windsor Park, attracting 17,961 spectators on 28th January with 'the only thing the most persistent grumbler could cavil at was the difficult approach to the enclosure'.

Some weeks after the international match, one aspect of the facilities fell short of basic requirements:

'It was demonstrated on Saturday that the Linfield people want conveniences erected inside their ground. I spoke before leaving the enclosure to one of the committee on the subject, and he was, strange to say, in entire accord

The Welsh team in front of the seated grand stand, 28th January 1911. The stand consists of a seated section at the rear and a standing enclosure at the front. The spectators are separated from the pitch side by a white picket fence

with my opinion on the subject. Let us hope these will materialise soon. They are already in evidence at all the other grounds.'

Demonstrating that it wasn't only available to host football matches, Windsor Park was used in May 1911 for a marching bands competition, which judging by the newspaper report was by then an annual event. In future years many such non-football events were held there, bringing extra revenue into Linfield's coffers:

'Great interest was manifested in the contests organised by the North of Ireland Flute, Brass, and Brass and Reed Bands' Association, which took place at Linfield Football grounds, Windsor Park, on Saturday afternoon. This was the fourth festival held under the auspices of the association, and both financially and otherwise it was perhaps the most successful. The open-air festival on Saturday was an entirely new departure. There was some doubt at the beginning to the measure of support it would receive from the public, but happily any misgivings on this score were removed when once the turnstiles at Windsor Park had been set in motion. An immense crowd of people paid for admission to the enclosure, and they all appeared to be keenly interested in the proceedings. In addition to the flute contests there were competitions for pipe bands, brass and brass and reed bands, and bugle bands. The weather was delightfully fine, and this fact no doubt tended to augment the attendance.'

Linfield continued to attract the crowds, especially to the occasional exhibition match.

Spectators in the standing enclosure, Linfield v Notts Forest exhibition match 1st January 1912

1912's Ireland v. England game was hosted at Dalymount Park, Dublin, with Windsor Park again hosting the Scots, in March:

'Great interest is being manifested in the international match between Ireland and Scotland which takes place to-day at Windsor Park, and a record attendance is anticipated. The Scottish team arrived yesterday morning, and are making their headquarters at Newcastle, County Down. A one-minute tram service will be run from Castle Junction, so that facilities for getting to the ground can be assured. Special excursions are being run on all the railways, and thousands of country visitors will be enabled to see the great international. The Edenderry Brass Band will render a choice selection of music at Windsor Park from 2.15. Sixteen turnstiles will be working, so that there will be no difficulty in gaining admission. The ground of Linfield is so enormous that it will accommodate 50,000. Everyone can have a good view of the match, and in the event of rain or inclement weather there is covered accommodation for over 12,000 to 15,000 people. The prices of admission are - unreserved 9d, reserved 1 shilling, grand stand 2 shillings. Anyone wishing to get to the grand stand pays 1s at turnstiles, and they can get in the stand by payment of another shilling.'

Poor weather however limited the attendance to around 12,000.

Initially Linfield were reluctant to host the game, as the IFA had sought to increase the levy they received from the gate from 10% to 20%. Linfield, supported by other clubs, held out and the IFA eventually relented.

The Linfield team of 1912/13 pictured in front of the south grand stand

First Ireland v England international at Windsor Park

In February 1913 Windsor Park finally got to host the prestigious Ireland v. England international match, and further improvements had been made to the accommodation, as the Northern Whig noted:

'The Linfield Club have made excellent arrangements for the match, and their new stand extension [presumed to be to the seated grand stand] will be opened for the first time. There will be covered seating accommodation for nearly 3,000 people, and in front of the stand there are eleven tiers 240 feet long under cover which will accommodate nearly 2,000.

On the unreserved side there is covered accommodation for nearly 5,000 people. On the unreserved side there will be nine stiles, seven at front entrance and two at Tate's Avenue entrance. Spectators coming by tram on Donegall Road route should get off at Donegall Avenue.

It is important that Linfield members should remember to show their tickets as otherwise they will not be admitted. Those desirous of gaining admission to grand stand enter by the 1s 6d stiles and then pass through the stile at stand paying 6d extra.

There are four stiles for entrance to the grand stand. The Sirocco Brass Band will render a selection of music from 2.15.

Special excursion trains are being run by all the railway companies. The prices of admission are unreserved 1s, reserved 1s 6d, grand stand 2s (pay 1s 6d at stile, and then pay 6d extra at grand stand). Ladies must pay, and there are no pass-out checks. All roads lead to Windsor Park on Saturday and, as this ground is capable of holding 40,000, we hope it will be taxed to its utmost. The kick-off is 3.30.'

This match saw Ireland's first ever victory over England (2-1), at the 32nd attempt. Newspaper estimates put the crowd figure between 21,000 and 22,000.

Building of the footbridge

The issue of access to the ground for large numbers of spectators had been a vexing one since Windsor Park had opened. The issue came to a head in 1913 and what follows is a transcript from a case taken by Linfield against the proposal by the Great Northern Railway (GNR) Company to build a footbridge over the railway line.

'Record Court before the Honourable Mr Justice Boyd.

ALLEGED INJURY TO FOOTBALL GROUND.

Claim by Linfield Club. The trustees the Linfield Football Club were the plaintiffs in a traverse case brought under the Great Northern Railway (Ireland) Acts, 1851, 1860 and 1864, against an award of £250. Plaintiffs held that the award was insufficient and that the amount should be £2,000.

The case for the traversers was that in 1904 the trustees acquired football premises which were contiguous to the city, and which had since been the venue of international and representative matches. A sum of £4,000 to £6,000 had been expended on the development and improvement of the grounds. The greater portion of the spectators were accustomed to come by the railway crossing at Windsor Avenue, and it was contended that the bridge which the railway company intended constructing in substitution for this level crossing would militate against the letting of the grounds for representative matches, and also would seriously affect the attendance at ordinary matches. It was estimated that a fifth to a sixth of the people would remain away from matches by reason of having to cross the railway lines by the bridge, and that the revenue would be diminished to that extent.

Arthur McDermott (treasurer of the club) and Joseph McBride gave evidence in support of the claim by the football club. The latter stated he was a member of the council of the Irish Football Association. Their committee had the selection of the ground on which international matches were to be played. The Linfield football ground was frequently selected for the purpose. He considered the proposed bridge would influence the attendance at the matches in the respect that a proportion of the visitors would be deterred from going owing to the risks when the crowd would be coming out.

Mr Chambers – What sort of a man would be deterred by a crush from going to a football match?

Witness – Women attended too.

Well, I will swear that a crush would not keep a woman away. A squeeze would not stop her (laughter). Are you the conjurer of fancied ill?

Nothing of the kind.

Are international matches ever played on any other ground in Belfast except Linfield?

Yes. Cliftonville, Distillery, and Glentoran. Have you ever been up at Winston's place - Paradise? (Laughter) [A reference to Winston Churchill, future UK Prime Minister, who had addressed a pro-Home Rule rally at Belfast Celtic's ground, known colloquially as "Paradise", in February 1912].

Mr Chambers – Yes.

Witness – Yes. There is a final tie there tomorrow.

Mr Chambers, addressing the jury, said no-one who knew him would accuse him of being wanting in sporting spirit or wanting in sympathy with any claim there might for the promotion of any means for the enjoyment of the public, but he did suggest to them that the award of the arbitrator - £250 - for the Linfield Football Club was far more than the justice of their case demanded.

Why did he say that? Because it was plain as daylight that when the alterations meditated by the railway company on the one hand and the City Corporation on the other were complete the Linfield club, as regarded the approaches to and exits from their ground, would be in a firmer position than ever before. He asked them, as sensible men, to consider the position of the club to-day. The only lawful approach to the ground was on an eight foot crossing over the railway, and thence to their ground over a twenty-foot way up to their gates. If a bridge had originally been in existence there and an attempt had been made to remove the bridge and substitute a level crossing he ventured to assert there was not an expert in Belfast - and experts were hardy fellows here - there was not one of them who would not have come trooping into the box and declared that in his opinion the Linfield Football Club was ruined for all time in the respect that the nervous and the halt - he was going to say the blind, though what would they be going to a football match for - would never go to the ground owing to the risks entailed.

Counsel referred to the number of trains which passed the point at certain hours of the day, and contended that the erection of the bridge would be a help rather than a hindrance for visitors to the Linfield Club's ground. No one, old or young, who wanted to attend a match on the ground would deterred by the fancied ills which had been conjured up by the various witnesses they had heard.

F. A. Campion, engineer for the Great Northern Railway Co; J. H. H. Swiney, C.E; and John Irwin, stationmaster, were examined. The last named stated that on the 15th February, the day of the English international, fifty-eight passenger trains, motors, and light engines had passed over the crossing at Windsor between 1 o'clock and 5.30 o'clock in the afternoon. That was the normal train service.

Mr Wilson – And 20,000 got into the football ground and there was no accident?

No.

Henry Thompson, ganger, said he often heard people passing to and repassing from the matches shouting to know why there was no footbridge.

Counsel – To whom were they shouting?

Witness – To everybody and to the man below (laughter).

Sergeant M'Kinley was examined as to police arrangements in the vicinity of the football grounds.

Mr Chambers – Have you ever heard prayers to somebody who lives downstairs to build a footbridge?

No.

Mr Chambers said there had been an obvious mistake in the award, and on the question both sides had come to an agreement, which was stated in the following terms:- "The Company agrees to the Linfield Football Club right of way for foot passengers and vehicles at all times over a road having an 18ft. carriageway, to be properly constructed and maintained by the company, on its own property, from Tate's Avenue to the 20th right of way granted to the club by the Trustees Suffern until such time as a public road be constructed from some point on Tate's Avenue which will give access to the 20th right of way.

In his address the jury his Lordship said it was a very exaggerated action on the part of the traversers. The claim was for an apprehended loss, not for one already sustained. He put it to the jury, which of them would like on a day when trains were going as frequently as had been deposed to in the evidence, and at a time when the crowd was leaving the grounds, which of them would prefer to cross the line by a level crossing or by a bridge. He never saw a case which was more fairly met by a railway company than that one, where the company's whole attitude had been "tell us what you want and we will do what we can." Could anything be fairer than that? The jury found for the traversers in £320. Judgment was given accordingly.'

Ireland won the British Home Championship for the first time in 1914, sealing this with the 1-1 draw versus Scotland at Windsor Park in March, 27,000 in attendance. The match was originally scheduled for Solitude but the Cliftonville club, recognising the importance of the game and the likelihood of an "abnormal" attendance, declined to host the game.

Later in the year, the 1913 court case settled, the GNR eventually got round to inviting contractors to construct the footbridge.

The Annual General Meeting of the GNR in 1916 reported 'the level crossings had been closed at Tate's Avenue and Lower Windsor Avenue, a wide footbridge having been substituted for the latter.'

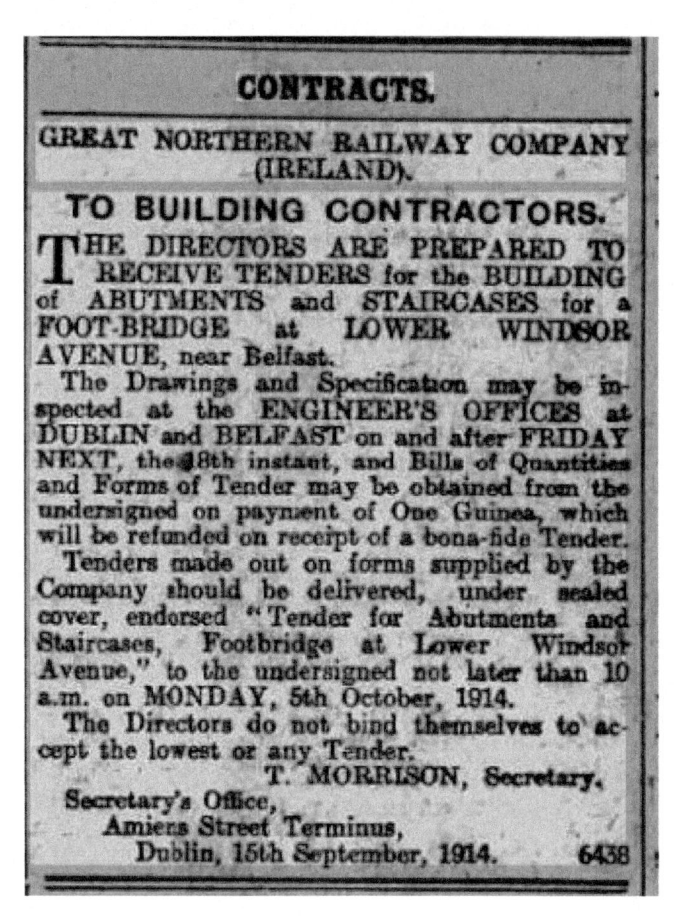

> **CONTRACTS.**
>
> **GREAT NORTHERN RAILWAY COMPANY (IRELAND).**
>
> **TO BUILDING CONTRACTORS.**
>
> THE DIRECTORS ARE PREPARED TO RECEIVE TENDERS for the BUILDING of ABUTMENTS and STAIRCASES for a FOOT-BRIDGE at LOWER WINDSOR AVENUE, near Belfast.
>
> The Drawings and Specification may be inspected at the ENGINEER'S OFFICES at DUBLIN and BELFAST on and after FRIDAY NEXT, the 18th instant, and Bills of Quantities and Forms of Tender may be obtained from the undersigned on payment of One Guinea, which will be refunded on receipt of a bona-fide Tender.
>
> Tenders made out on forms supplied by the Company should be delivered, under sealed cover, endorsed "Tender for Abutments and Staircases, Footbridge at Lower Windsor Avenue," to the undersigned not later than 10 a.m. on MONDAY, 5th October, 1914.
>
> The Directors do not bind themselves to accept the lowest or any Tender.
>
> T. MORRISON, Secretary.
> Secretary's Office,
> Amiens Street Terminus,
> Dublin, 15th September, 1914. 6438

The Great War

International games were suspended during the 1914-1918 Great War. The Irish League, too, was suspended and a Belfast and District league introduced for the 1915-16 season, played by six teams (Linfield won), though crowds were down - a Linfield clash against Belfast Celtic in September 1914 saw a reduction in takings of £112 from the previous season. The Great War also saw large numbers of players and supporters joining up for active service, and it was estimated that at least 4,000 Linfield supporters were 'in khaki' by April 1915.

As part of the war effort, in 1917 Windsor Park hosted a baseball game between teams made up of US and Canadian soldiers and ex-pats living in London.

A report of a 1917 Linfield versus Glentoran match commented on the large crowds – and the unorthodox means used by some spectators to get to the ground:

'The road to Windsor Park on Saturday was reminiscent of International contests, all sorts of vehicles besides trams being pressed into use. One small pony and miniature jaunting car, loaded with enthusiasts shouting "Go on the Greens" evoking more than passing interest. And the closely-packed ranks of spectators in the ample enclosure put the finishing touch to the idea, for outside an Irish Cup final or the battle for the Steel & Sons' Cup there has been no larger gathering of late years to witness a football game in the city.'

After the Great War was over, international fixtures resumed, with the first such match in over five years taking place at Windsor Park between Ireland and England on 25th October 1919:

'Every Ford in Ulster was called into action' a reporter identified only as 'Celt', told readers of the Irish News and Belfast Morning News. 'Brakes, char-a-bancs, every kind of vehicle down to a fish-cart, which I saw come down York Street at noon, emptied sporting Ulster into the city. The morning trains were packed. It was the biggest invasion of country sports in the history of Irish football.'

Trams were also said to be running to the stadium at half-minute intervals. By the time the match got under way at around 3.15pm, some 40,000 were jammed into the ground.

The footbridge over the railway

6

Turnstiles

'Ellison's Rush Preventive Turnstiles'

The first report of the installation of mechanical turnstiles at a British football ground was as Hampden Park, Glasgow in 1873. These replaced the 'open gate' system which often saw operators overwhelmed by the numbers of spectators trying to get into matches.

The means of controlling access to paying customers was relatively straightforward, consisting of a cast iron heavyweight barrier controlled by an operator once the relevant entrance fee had been paid. Club owners were also aware that 'gate' receipts often fell below crowd estimates, leading to suspicions that some gate operators were 'on the take'.

To combat this, in 1895 the firm of W.T. Ellison, based in the small town of Irlams o' Th' Heights, near Manchester, launched their patented 'Ellison's Rush Preventive Turnstiles'. These included a sealed in, tamper-proof 'incrometer' (counter) to record the numbers of people entering each gate; and a foot pedal that allowed the operator to lock and unlock the rotating gate as each entrant paid and passed through. They were designed to safely admit up to 4,000 spectators per hour, reduced to 3,000 if change needed to be given. Almost every major sports ground in the UK installed these turnstiles, including Wembley Stadium, Twickenham and Murrayfield, as well as clubs in Ireland including Distillery, Cliftonville and Glentoran.

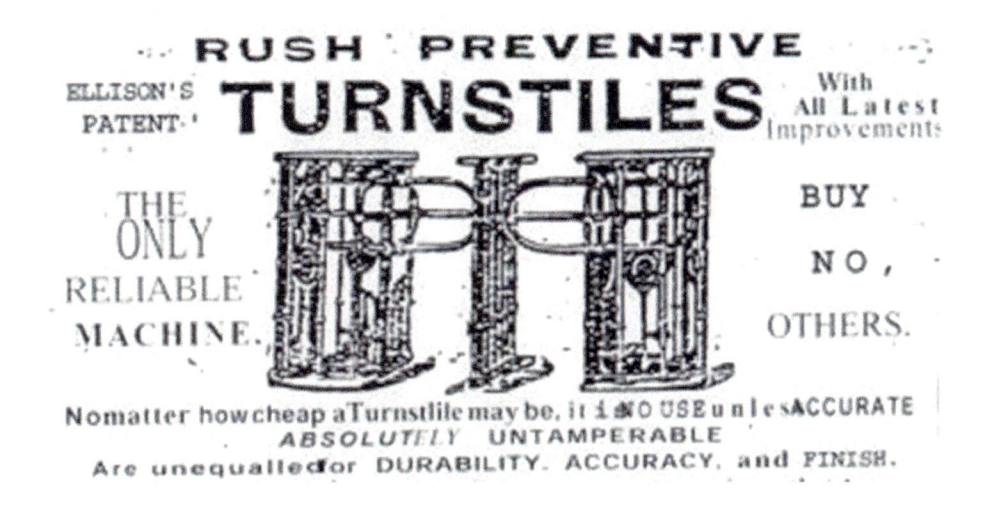

Windsor Park was no exception, and the continued growth in (and need to control) large crowds led Linfield to build new entrances, opened in 1923:

New entrance and turnstiles, 1923

The turnstiles used were supplied by Ellison's. During the rebuilding of Windsor Park in 2015 a number of these were uncovered, long disused, in one of the old entrances to the unreserved terraces:

Original "rush preventive" Windsor Park turnstiles uncovered during the 2015 rebuild at an entrance on Olympia Drive

One of these originals was reclaimed and restored and is now on display in the IFA Education and Heritage Centre at Windsor Park:

Windsor Park turnstile preserved in the IFA Education and Heritage Centre

The brass inlay into which the automatic ceramic counter was sealed with lead

7

1920s

Football, boxing, athletics, rugby, and speedway

Throughout the decade Windsor Park hosted a variety of non-football sporting events as well as other social gatherings. The marching bands contests 'for brass, brass and reed, flute, pipe and bugle bands' continued as they had done pre-war.

Boxing

Amateur boxing bouts were common in the 1920s:

'BOXING AT WINDSOR PARK [1920]

A fine tribute was paid to the popularity of Bob Nixon, a former Linfield player, at Windsor Park yesterday afternoon, when a boxing tournament was held with the object of raising funds to help him in the trying period which he has experienced as a result of his withdrawal from the football arena owing to the accident that befell him two or three years ago. The attendance exceeded expectations. All the Belfast sportsmen seemed to make Windsor Park their venue, and they were rewarded by witnessing a capital afternoon's sport. The ring was located on a platform which had been erected under the grandstand cover, and spectators in all parts of the field were thus able to get good view of the contests.'

'The Linfield Executive wind up their [1921] summer programme of boxing to-day with a bill of eight contests - a scheduled 75 rounds - and have three stand by bouts. They guarantee at least three hours boxing. There is covered accommodation for 6,000 patrons, and the bill goes on no matter the weather conditions.'

Photos of boxing bouts in 1924

Athletics

Athletics meetings were also held in the summer months. The 1921 newspaper advertisement below was for a Triangular International athletics meeting. Eric Liddell, whose story featured in the 1980's film 'Chariots of Fire', won the 100 yards sprint race. Athletics meetings would continue to be held up to the 1950s.

> **FRIDAY, JULY 8, 1921.**
>
> **IRISH AMATEUR ATHLETIC ASSOCIATION.**
>
> **"A DAY OF DAYS."**
>
> **INTERNATIONAL CONTEST**
>
> AT
>
> **WINDSOR PARK, BELFAST,**
>
> SATURDAY, 9th July, at 3 p.m.
>
> ENGLAND,
>
> IRELAND,
>
> SCOTLAND.
>
> ALL THE CHAMPIONS OF THE THREE COUNTRIES APPEAR.
> NOTHING LIKE THIS MEETING EVER WITNESSED IN BELFAST.
> BALMORAL BRASS BAND WILL PERFORM.
> Admission—2s and 1s (including tax).

Rugby

In 1922 a rugby union inter-provincial match between Ulster and Leinster was played at Windsor Park, as was the final of the Ulster School's Cup, an annual rugby union tournament for Northern Irish schools, held at Windsor Park for the only time. Campbell College Belfast beat Royal Belfast Academical Institute 10-0.

Social events included gatherings of Boy Scouts, the Boys Brigade and other organisations:

> 'ORDER OF RECHABITES. THE GOAL OF PROHIBITION.
>
> On Saturday a demonstration of the Belfast lodges connected with the Independent Order of Rechabites was held at Windsor Park (kindly lent for the occasion by the directors and committee of Linfield FC). It was the first of the kind during the past six years, and was most successful. An imposing procession was made to the meeting place via Bedford Street, Howard Street, Great Victoria Street, Sandy Row, Donegall Rood, and Donegall Avenue. The procession had included in it a number of striking tableaux conveying the lesson of temperance, and these were the object of much admiration.'

However these were testing times in Ireland. The Home Rule crisis had dogged Irish politics for decades, with nationalists seeking to govern the affairs of Ireland from a parliament in Dublin, and unionists resisting this notion. Football suffered as a result and there were a number of instances of riots at grounds in Belfast, with reports of shots being fired at matches in the early 1920s. The solution to the Irish question as proposed by the Liberal government in London, was to partition the island and give both units a limited form of self-government.

During the Great War, football leagues in Ireland had operated on an unofficial, regional basis. However, a dispute arose over where the March 1921 Irish Cup semi-final reply between northern club Glenavon and Dublin side Shelbourne should be played. The first tie, a draw, had been played at a neutral venue in Belfast.

Although convention indicated that the replayed game should be played in Dublin, the Belfast-based IFA dictated that the replay should take place in Belfast. Glenavon players were wary of travelling to Dublin at a time of great political and civil unrest; Shelbourne refused to travel again to Belfast for similar reasons and forfeited the tie.

Two weeks later the "Football Association of Ireland" was created by the Leinster FA on behalf of the southern based clubs.

The IFA, however, continued to organise an international team to play in the Home international series, as "Ireland", and to run the annual Irish Cup competition. A large crowd had attended the Ireland versus Scotland game at Windsor Park in February 1921.

Partition led to much violence across the island of Ireland, and over 450 people were killed in Belfast from 1920 to 1922. In December 1921 in Armagh an IRA Unit opened fire on a train carrying the Linfield team.

Fans packed into the unreserved terracing, Ireland v. Scotland 1921. Some spectators have touchline 'seats'

The cover over the unreserved side provided a great vantage point. An estimated 30,000 attended v. Scotland 1921.

Linfield cemented their position as the most successful club by winning seven trophies in the 1921/22 season, losing only one game, and were to follow this with League and Cup doubles in 1922/23 and 1929/30.

In March 1925 a new crowd record was recorded:

> 'Over 40,000 spectators saw Ireland's Association football team beaten at Windsor Park, Belfast, Saturday, the conquerors being the Scottish. Ireland's hopes of success in the soccer match were not high; we had not beaten Scotland since 1910. But so feeble was the display put up at Windsor Park that an exodus from the grounds commenced at half-time. The final score was three goals to nil for the visitors.'

> '[The match was attended by] a crowd that equalled almost one-tenth of the population of Belfast. It is difficult to repel a feeling of pessimism over present-day Irish international football. I have seen a good few of these contests in my time, and am open to confess that the great majority of the recent games have not been worth – well, getting the breathe squeezed out of one's body going over Windsor bridge.'

The 1925 crowd versus Scotland take up vantage points on top of the pavilion at the railway end of the ground

1927 was to see the first Irish victory over England at Windsor Park. For the much anticipated occasion, a special addition was made to the ground:

'His Grace the Duke of Abercorn, Governor Northern Ireland, and his party will be accommodated with a special stand erected in front of the Linfield Pavilion. Many improvements have been made to the ground since last year, the greatest of which is the banking up of the big space on the near left hand or reserved side. This has been done in such a way that the spectators will be standing in single rows rising higher and higher back to the paling. I deliberately viewed the Linfield v Larne match on Saturday from this corner, and saw every kick of the game.'

Access to the seated grand stand was by pre-purchased ticket only; all other spectators would pay cash at the turnstiles:

'Unparalleled interest is being taken in the [Ireland v. England] clash. So much so, indeed, on the other side of the Channel that over 2,000 spectators are coming from the Midlands of England, having chartered three special steamers to bring them across. All the stand seats were gobbled up by a hungry public on this side within a few hours after being advertised, and it looks like favourable weather alone is needed to establish a new attendance record.

There will be twenty-seven turnstiles in operation, that there should be no undue or long waiting outside the grounds. Of these, seventeen, at suitable places, will serve the unreserved, and the other ten the reserved. Holders of tickets for touchline seats will enter by a special gate.'

Composite photograph taken from a 1927 newsreel of Ireland v. England showing the original south grand stand. The newly banked mound is to the left of the stand. Note the two policemen on the roof, posted there to deter enthusiasts. The spire of Windsor Presbyterian Church on the Lisburn Road is just visible through the mist

'Invariably fortunate with regard to weather, the Irish Football Association on this occasion were disappointed, for the rain which commenced to fall on Friday morning continued without intermission during the whole of the day and night until Saturday evening. This factor probably reduced the attendance by about 10,000, but nevertheless there was a gathering of over 30,000 people, the great majority of whom had no cover of any kind.

Special trains brought many enthusiasts to the city from all parts of the country, and these were amongst the earliest arrivals at Windsor Park, where those who had not been fortunate to obtain tickets sought the shelter of the covered stands on both sides of the enclosure. Most to be pitied were the party of 2,000 trippers from the English Midlands, who crossed from England on three special steamers on Friday night, and had experienced nothing but rain from the time they left their homes in the Notts and Derby district. They had been provided with touchline seats, the first occasion in recent years when the IFA has made arrangements of this kind, and these hardy miners had an unenviable experience of sitting out in the open, and with little cause for enthusiasm in respect of the team which they had hoped to cheer to victory. Many of the seats provided for their accommodation were unoccupied, and no wonder, for at the mountain end of the ground the track was several inches deep in water, and the boys who eventually took possession of the seats sat with their feet drawn up in the tailor fashion, and were afforded some shelter from the elements by the spectators outside the railings.

One's sympathies also went out to the four stalwart members of the Royal Ulster Constabulary who had been detailed for duty on the top of each stand, presumably with the object of restraining those keen enthusiasts who on international days, scale to the roof of the stands to get a bird's eye view of the game. Their duties were light, but uncomfortable on this occasion… It was a dull, dispirited crowd until the appearance of the teams roused them, and then once the game got under way the enthusiasm blazed and was maintained at fever heat until the close of the memorable contest.

Young supporters revelling in the mud in front of The Kop, 1927

Itinerant musicians, instrumental and vocal, were everywhere, and the band of the Grosvenor Hall very appropriately included a medley of sea songs in their programme.'

Ireland beat England that day, 2-0 but lost the fixture against Wales, so failed to win the Championship outright. There would not be another victory over the English in Belfast until 2005.

Speedway

The sport of speedway spread throughout the UK in 1928, and was briefly trialled at Windsor Park. A track was situated around the pitch and it was intended to use this track to hold dirt-track racing. However the Ulster Centre of the Motorcycle Union of Ireland, concerned about the possible effect on the number of entrants in other branches of the sport, were not impressed by the idea and refused to issue a permit.

Despite that, on the 29th September a meeting did take place promoted by the British Dirt-Track Racing Association, but the Ulster Centre did not relent and the riders who participated were suspended and fined a £1 for taking part in the unauthorised meeting.

Speedway track being laid, 1928

'Some four thousand people saw dirt-track, or speedway, motor cycle racing for the first time at Windsor Park, Belfast, Saturday afternoon, when the British Dirt-Track Racing Association held its first meeting there. Twenty races were run off in a little over two hours.'

A second and final speedway race meeting took place on Saturday 6th October 1928.

WINDSOR PARK - A History of the Home of Linfield FC & Northern Ireland

Football, of course, continued to be the main sport. Newsreel images from the 1929 Irish Cup semi-final between Coleraine and Ballymena give a good sense of the ground at that time:

A view of the teams emerging from the Pavilion at the railway end of the ground. This photo and those that follow are from newsreel film of the 1929 Irish Cup semi-final between Coleraine and Ballymena

A long view of the railway end, with the spire of St Thomas' Church of Ireland church, Lisburn Road, in the distance

A steam train thunders by in the distance on the GNR railway line. Notice how far back from the touchline the terraces are. They have not yet been "lowered", that was to follow in 1937

A new stand

Later in 1929 Linfield began the erection of an annex/extension to the south grand stand. It is not known how the decision to build this came about; presumably it was in response to the ever increasing crowds attending football matches and other sporting and social events – and perhaps Linfield's desire to continue to catch the eye of the IFA when local representative matches and international games were being allocated. It is also not clear why opportunity wasn't taken to build a new single structure on the entire length of the south stand – perhaps funds were limited? As it happened, Linfield embarked on yet further improvements less than a year later, with funds to be raised through a year-long campaign. The Belfast News Letter carried a lengthy report on the stand's construction in August 1929:

'BUILDING AND ENGINEERING.

The above photograph shows the fine new stand which has been erected at Windsor Park, Belfast, the headquarters of the Linfield Football Club. This stand will seat more than 2,000 people, and will add very considerably to the amenities of the ground, already regarded as the best football enclosure in the North of Ireland.

The new stand has been placed at the railway end of the old [south] stand, and the two stands together extend from one end of the playing pitch to the other.

The history of the new stand is not without interest, in view of to-day's great event on the Ards circuit. For last year's race a stand was put up at Cree's Corner and another at Dundonald, but the owners decided not to repeat their experiment this year. The Linfield Club thereupon bought the timber, and the stands were dismantled and the material transported to Windsor Park. Mr Kendrick Edwards, M.lnst.C.E., F.R.I.B.A. of Scottish Temperance Buildings, Belfast, was appointed to prepare a scheme for the erection and roofing of the stand, and after he had done so, the contract for the construction of the stand was given to Messrs. Agnew & Co., Parkgate Avenue, Belfast, and Messrs. Musgrave Co., Ltd., of St. Ann's Ironworks, Belfast, were given the contract for the supply and erection of the steelwork.

The new stand has nineteen rows of seats, steeply sloped, and it affords a splendid view of all parts of the ground. The old stand has only eight rows of seats, and care had to be taken that the line of vision of spectators occupying it should not be interfered with by the new stand, which is much higher and projects much further towards the playing pitch railings than the older erection. That difficulty has been successfully overcome.

The foundations of the new stand are all of concrete, and in every respect it is a very solid structure. There will be six entrances, three in front, and three giving access to the centre of the stand from a passageway underneath the seats, entered by a doorway in the railway end of the erection.

The most interesting feature of the job is the steel roofwork, an impressive expanse which catches the eye at once. The spread of steelwork measures 59ft. 1in. across and 178 ft. in length, to the point where it joins the older stand. The front portion of the roof is cantilevered, so that there are no uprights to interfere with the view of spectators. The roof as a whole is

The extension to the south grand stand nearing completion. The curved roof of the original 1909 grand stand is just visible to the right of the new stand

supported on centre and back columns, and the braced cantilevers which support the front portion have a span of 27ft. from the centre columns and a centre latticed girder. The back portion of the roof is supported on girders similar to those employed on the front portion, but it is carried to back columns and centre columns, the latter at 30ft centres. A rolled steel stringer tie has been placed at each of the centre columns underneath the stand. The steel roof has been sheeted over and covered with a felt roofing material.

The use of the cantilever principle for a steel roof of these dimensions is not unique, but there are not a great many examples of the use of the method, and this is the first one in Northern Ireland. The successful way in which the engineering problems been overcome reflect credit on Mr. Edwards and Messrs. Musgrave, who are specialists in structural steelwork, and have carried this difficult contract in a thoroughly satisfactory manner, in keeping with their reputation.

The general contractors Messrs. Agnew have provided a thoroughly good job and carried out the contract in the shortest possible time. Work was begun at the end of the last football season and the stand is now practically completed.

The roofing material was supplied and manufactured by a Belfast firm, and the Linfield Club must be congratulated on having relied on local work for every part of the scheme.'

The new stand was known colloquially as the 'Balmoral' Stand.

In October 1929, Linfield installed a scoreboard spectators could see the latest scores in other games being played by checking against the letters on the board that corresponded with the relevant code letter for the games listed in the match day programme:

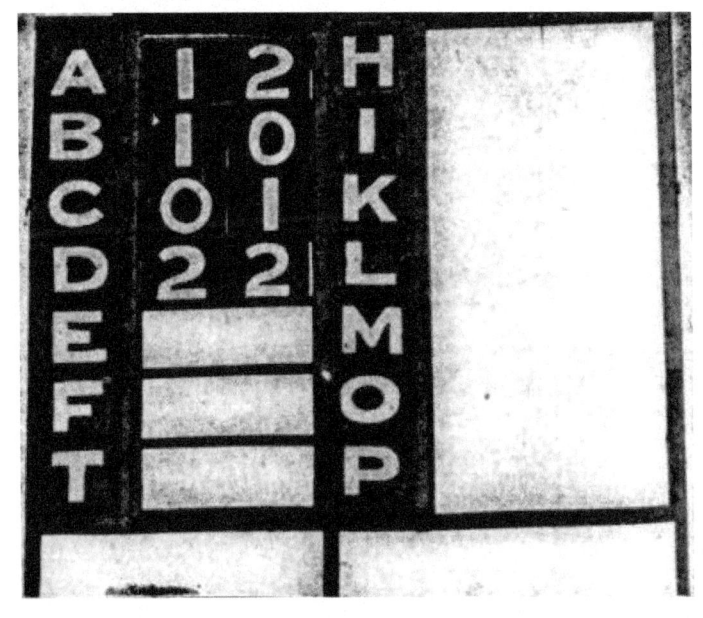

The decade closed with Windsor Park established as the premier ground for football in Northern Ireland. It had come a long way from its opening in 1905 to becoming, little over 20 years later, a ground capable of hosting a variety of events and football crowds around the 40,000 mark. Linfield had driven and paid for these improvements, the need for which was often made by both the desire to accommodate larger crowds and to compete with the other major grounds in Belfast (and, pre the political partition of Ireland in 1921, in Dublin) to become the first choice venue for hosting prestigious – and lucrative – local representative and international matches.

Linfield didn't yet have exclusivity on hosting international games – Belfast's Celtic Park would continue to host the odd international up until 1936, and Irish Cup finals were played at venues at Cliftonville, Glentoran and Belfast Celtic so as to be "neutral" for the finalists each year – but they were well on the way.

8

1930s

Archibald Leitch's grand stand

Linfield continued to undertake significant works to improve facilities at Windsor Park, with the two most notable projects of the decade being the building of a new grand stand and pavilion in 1930, and the increasing of the terraced parts of the ground in 1937. By the end of the decade, the ground was essentially complete in the form that endured until the early 1980's. The area around Windsor Park expanded, too, with dozens of red brick terraced houses built to the east of the unreserved cover, which thereafter took its new name from the closest street – Olympia Drive.

The building of the new grand stand on the south side of the ground in 1930 was a significant move to increase the covered seated capacity and the stand remained, more or less, in its original situation until its demolition in 2014. Its design was by Archibald Leitch of Glasgow, doyen of stadiums built all over the UK. In truth, it was a simple enough, almost copycat design, bearing more than a passing resemblance to other, grander, Leitch stands at places such as Ibrox Park and Stamford Bridge. Using Leitch to produce essentially an off-the-shelf stand design perhaps explains why the new stand

Leitch's sketch for the new grand stand

somewhat uncomfortably adjoined the 'Balmoral' stand constructed just one year previously. The front rows of seating within the new 1929 stand had to be removed to ensure the two stands were aligned (providing '4,500 comfy seats'), and the new stand was designed to contain dressing rooms, club offices and other ancillary facilities.

The old, 1909 stand still had a life, as the roof was repositioned at the railway end of the ground, covering a new standing enclosure that replaced the old pavilion and press room. That roof would stay in place until its eventual demolition in 2010. Aerial photographs from later years reveal that the roof re-erected at the railway end was not quite perpendicular to the pitch, sloping inwards from the south-east to north-east corners.

To obtain the necessary finances for the design and building costs of the new stand Linfield formed a Pavilion Fund committee, with the express aim of raising £10,000 – a huge sum, equating to over £650,000 in 2020 terms.

In February 1930, a local newspaper reported that 'The scheme for the erection of a new pavilion at Windsor Park, Belfast – the headquarters of the Linfield Football Club – is being pushed on rapidly. Plans are in preparation, and it is expected that tenders will be asked at the end of March, so as to permit of work being begun at the close of the present playing season and completed before the opening of the next one.

The proposed pavilion will be more in keeping with the ground and the position of the Linfield Club than the present wooden structure. It will be a two-storey building, of brick, with a wood verandah which will command a fine view of the playing pitch. The accommodation will comprise a board room, a reception-room, with a spacious entrance hall. The accommodation in the way of baths will be extensive and thoroughly up-to-date. The pavilion will be electrically lighted and there will be a heating chamber below ground level.

The project for the erection of this pavilion has been energetically taken up by the Linfield Supporters' Club, who have already a considerable sum of money in hand towards the cost of the scheme.'

Linfield players, too, played their part in the fund raising, and later that month it was reported that a 'splendidly patronised' carnival dance raised £150. The prizes for costumes were presented by Linfield's famous and popular centre forward, Joe Bambrick.

Work got underway with serious intent at the end of the footballing season in May 1930, with the arrival of the steel work.

'Messrs. W. Miskimmon & Son, McTeir Street, Belfast, have been given the contract for the erection of the new stand to be built at Windsor Park, Belfast, for the Linfield Football Club. Messrs. Musgrave and Co., Belfast, are to supply the steel work. The new stand will be on the reserved side of the ground, and will extend from the stand erected last year. It will take the place of the old wooden stand now remaining. The roof of that stand will be removed to the railway end of the ground, and will form a covering over a steep terrace. Cover will thus be provided for a length of 72 yards and considerable accommodation will be available on ground now occupied by the existing pavilion.

The new stand will be able to seat a large number of people, who will enter the ground by separate turnstiles and gain access to the stand from the rear. Accommodation—with tip-up seats—will be reserved for directors and officials of the home and visiting clubs and for representatives of the Press. The pavilion accommodation will be below the stand. The main entrance will be at one end and a corridor will extend below the structure, with all the rooms opening off it. The accommodation will include directors room, offices, cloak-rooms, etc., and extensive provision will be made for players, who will have slipper baths and plunge baths. Electric light will be installed and a hot water heating system will be installed.

The stand will be backed by a brick wall. The seats will be of wood, and a truss roof will be covered with asbestos tiles. The competing teams will pass to and from the playing pitch by way of a corridor passing to the front of the stand. Another improvement will be the banking of the ground between the railings and the stand. This scheme, which will make Windsor Park the best equipped football enclosure in Ireland, has been prepared by Messrs, Leech [sic] & Partners, civil engineers, Glasgow.'

Work continued apace over the summer of 1930. In July, the newspapers were reporting progress on the new structure as well as some other improvements around the ground: 'Considerable progress has been made with the new stands and dressing rooms at Windsor Park. Where the old pavilion stood [at the railway end] a large stand is in course of erection. This should house several thousand spectators under cover, a big asset when the weather is bad. The new structure is being erected from the woodwork of the old reserved stand, with new iron frame work set in concrete blocks. At the new stand erected last year the front tier of seats have been removed to keep it in line with the additional stand and dressing rooms. As the iron work is erected the wooden tiers are being put in position. The brick work of the dressing rooms is also going on at the same time. A large number of workmen are engaged night and day to have all in readiness for the beginning of the football season. The unreserved terracing has been greatly improved, and the playing pitch has been specially treated.'

By August, local journalists were providing extensive coverage of the new construction: 'The dressing rooms and stands are progressing rapidly, workmen being engaged on them till dark each night. The plunge baths are being laid in the dressing rooms, but in my opinion they might have been constructed on a larger scale.'

'The Linfield club has many alterations made to the enclosure since last season, due to the enthusiasm displayed by the supporters club, headed by Alderman Harry Midgley, MP [later to be Linfield chairman]. The old stand which adjoined the new one on the reserved side is away, and in its steed is a new and palatial structure. Under it are the new club dressing rooms, and the offices of the club. The old reserved stand has been erected behind what was the pavilion goal. Linfield are a wonderful go-ahead club.'

'WINDSOR PARK STAND. Linfield Club's £10,000 Scheme Nearing Completion. 2,500 EXTRA SEATS.

Operations on the new £10,000 stand and dressing rooms for Linfield Football Club at Windsor Park, Belfast, are nearing completion, and the opening ceremony takes place on 15th September. Amongst the novel features introduced in the stand, which is of steel construction with truss roof principle and a brick wall along the back ten feet high, are tip-up seats. These will accommodate the home and visiting directors and Press representatives, and the improvement will provide 2,500 extra seats, making with the existing accommodation 4,200 stand seats. The old reserved stand has been re-erected along the railway end of the ground, and will afford cover for 6,000 spectators, so that cover is now provided for 25,000 spectators, and the holding capacity of the ground is estimated at 50,000.

Opening off the main entrance is a corridor leading to the official rooms, which are all laid out underneath the stand. These comprise board, tea and checker's rooms and secretary's office, with inquiry bureau, lavatories, and referee's quarters—which have been equipped with a bath, & WC. Up-to-date dressing-rooms for the home and visiting team have also been provided. The home pavilion contains dressing-room, plunge and shower baths, two slipper baths, and three wash hand basins and lavatories, while the visitors' quarters embrace similar facilities. The bath rooms are all tiled, and a boiler house and trainer's room have also been arranged on modern lines. In addition, ladies and gentlemen's cloakrooms have been constructed underneath the old stand, and the rooms will also be heated, the new premises being lighted by electricity throughout. The architects were Messrs. Archibald Leitch & Partners of London and Glasgow, who have been responsible for the design of virtually all the football grounds in England and Scotland.'

WINDSOR PARK - A History of the Home of Linfield FC & Northern Ireland

Original 'Bennet' tip-up seats in the central section of the grand stand, shortly before demolition in 2014

Bench seats in the new grand stand

Bennet "tip up" seats

The company responsible for the new stand and pavilion, Archibald Leitch of Glasgow, brought a lot of business to Bennet of Glasgow, makers of tip-up wooden seats. Bennet seats were durable and designed so that they could be easily replaced if broken or damaged. Leitch designed his seating decks with seat widths of 18 inches, which was three inches more than the standard set by train and omnibus companies. That same measurement – 460mm – is still used today in stadia, albeit as a minimum.

It is highly likely that the tip-up seats installed in the South Stand in 1930 were of this design and from this supplier. There were originally 590 of these tip-up seats, located in the middle section of the stand. All other seats were of the bench type, although spaces on these were also individually numbered. These original tip-up seats remained in the stand until its demolition in 2014.

The first competitive match played in front of the new stand was Linfield v. Belfast Celtic, 23rd August 1930, Celtic winning 2-0. A journalist report of that game was particular in its description of facilities for the press:

'First of all, I must congratulate all concerned for the magnificent improvements that have been made to the Windsor Park enclosure. The new stand gives the ground an entirely new appearance, and it would compare favourably with any ground I have visited across the water. There is an unfortunate band of human beings generally referred to as reporters, and so long as they do their work few seem to mind or care under what conditions it is done. Time and again I have had to fight my way into a seat in the Press box (so-called) at different grounds, because every Tom, Dick, and Harry was allowed to occupy seats supposed to be reserved for the Press. Therefore it was very satisfactory to find that the Linfield Club had provided most excellent accommodation. Every scribe has a turn-up seat to himself, and an excellent view of the game. It is true he is right in the midst of raucous voices calling on their favourites "Play up", "Slip it to Joe", "For goodness sake go off", or else giving free advice to the referee and telling him his character in unmistakable fashion, but reporters, like sailors, don't care. A study of a football crowd is a most interesting one, provided one has a sense of humour. The vast majority can see only one team, and when their favourites bring down a man it is a case of "That's the stuff to give 'em", but when the other fellow retaliates he is a dirty dog who ought to be suspended for life. Ah, well, as some philosopher once remarked: "Men are only boys grown tall.'

The new grand stand ready to open, 1930. Note the rough ground at the Kop end and the basic terracing in the corner

The official opening, 15th September 1930

The extension was officially opened on Monday September 15th 1930 with a match between Glasgow Rangers and Linfield. The advert for the game detailed that proceeds would go to the Pavilion Fund.

```
DO IT NOW.  DON'T BE LATE.
GET YOUR GRAND STAND
        TICKET NOW
            FOR THE
    GLASGOW RANGERS
              v.
         LINFIELD
   MATCH AT WINDSOR PARK ON
  MONDAY, 15th SEPTEMBER,
        AT 6.30 O'CLOCK.
    PROCEEDS FOR PAVILION FUND.
 Members are respectfully asked to pay.
 Tickets on Sale at City Shops and from the
            Club Secretary.
      YOUR SEAT GUARANTEED.
   UNRESERVED ........ SIXPENCE
   RESERVED .......... ONE SHILLING
   GRAND STAND ....... TWO SHILLINGS
    No Tickets on Sale after Saturday next.
         4,500 COMFY SEATS.
     A GLORIOUS VIEW OF THE GAME,
    AND THE OPENING CEREMONY OF
              NEW STAND, &c.
```

The Rangers officials – including architect Archibald Leitch – and team members were given a pre-match civic welcome at Belfast's City Hall by the Lord Mayor, followed by a wreath laying by the Rangers captain at the Cenotaph, and visits to local mills.

Glasgow Rangers in Belfast

Glasgow Rangers Football Team at the City Hall, where they were received by the Right Hon. the Lord Mayor.—(Left to Right) Mr. A. Leitch (Architect); Mr. W. Struth (Manager); Sir William Coates, Bart.; Mr. J. Bowie (Director), and Mr. R. J. Campbell (Director).

The match itself kicked off at 6.30pm, with the opening ceremony at half-time being curtailed somewhat due to fading light. The game finished 0-0, in near-darkness:

'By this time [second half] the light was fading rapidly, and a wag in front of the stand caused some merriment, wondering in loud voice 'whether the referee had got one of them illuminated watches.' The pace was faster now, but play was difficult to follow in the growing twilight. It did not matter a great deal, however, as neither side managed to score.'

OPENING OF NEW PAVILION AND DRESSING-ROOMS AT WINDSOR PARK, BELFAST.—GLASGOW RANGERS PLAYED LINFIELD A FRIENDLY GAME, THE RESULT BEING A SCORELESS DRAW. (LEFT TO RIGHT) T. CRAIG (CAPTAIN, RANGERS), J. SAUNDERSON (REFEREE), T. SLOAN (CAPTAIN, LINFIELD) AND SIR ROBERT BAIRD, D.L., WHO DECLARED THE PAVILION OPEN AND ALSO KICKED-OFF.

The official kick-off. The original grand stand roof, re-erected at the railway end, can be seen at the top right

A celebration dinner was given after the match, in Thompsons Restaurant, Donegall Place, Belfast, when the Glasgow Rangers' team and officials of the club and large company of guests were entertained It was disclosed that during the past eight years Linfield Club had expended £22,000 in improving and equipping their grounds – equivalent to a staggering £1.3 million in 2020 terms. At the dinner, Sir Robert Baird [Linfield] recalled the early days of Linfield when 'The Meadow' behind Linfield Mill provided the pitch. He said: 'have we not yet a ground here equal to Ibrox Park we are going as near it as possible. Perhaps someday - for Linfield is not finished yet - we may have the pleasure of asking our Glasgow friends over and able to point to this enclosure and say 'What better have you at your place!'

The new pavilion allowed the teams to enter the playing field directly from underneath the new grand stand via a 'tunnel'.

Brickwork in the tunnel under the 1930 stand leading to the original dressing rooms

Ireland v. England 1935 showing the teams emerging from the tunnel leading directly from the south grand stand

Linfield also improved the entrance to the reserved enclosure by planting shrubs and trees on the inclines and along the entire avenue at the back of the grandstand.

The decade was also a successful one for Linfield on the pitch as the team won four league titles and five Irish Cups.

Windsor Park hosted friendly ties for Linfield against quality opposition, including Manchester City, Chelsea, Sheffield Wednesday and Leicester City. A match against West Bromwich Albion was played in May 1932 to help raise funds to pay off debt from erecting the grandstand, 10,000 attending. At a game against the Austrian side Sports Club Saaz, Vienna, in January 1934, it was reported that 'prior to the start, the Saaz team gave their national salute.'

In 1931 an approach from a local syndicate to rent or lease Windsor Park for greyhound racing 'on terms which were most generous from a financial point of view' was rejected by the Linfield Committee, who had faced calls from local church leaders for Linfield to maintain their firm stand on hosting only 'clean and manly sports', and not introduce any sport that 'is openly associated with gambling.'

Despite the improvements, a serious 'gate crashing' incident occurred at the 1936 Ireland v Scotland match:

'10,000 SOCCER GATE-CRASHERS AT WINDSOR. THE NATIONAL ANTHEM AVERTS POSSIBLE DISASTER.

The game was played in a unique and somewhat dangerous setting. The gates had to be closed ten minutes before the kick-off, but thousands, undeterred, broke in and swarmed right up to the touchlines, and could not be dislodged.

There was a thrilling and unforgettable sight just prior to the kick-off. All pushing and excited commotion on the touchlines came to a dead stop as if by magic, and harassed officials, police and crowd that was well out of hand uncovered and stood like statues when the band of the Border Regiment struck up the National Anthem.

It might appropriately enough be added here that the official attendance was returned at 40,000. That is to say that number paid for admission, but nearer 50,000 was present. It was obvious, however, that the gate crashers did not want to avoid payment. Many of them had travelled long distances and simply took the main chance when a double entrance gate went down, only to discover that there was no possible room for them inside the barriers. What the receipts would have amounted to had all been able to gain admission through the automatic turnstiles it is difficult to hazard a guess. As it was, a new record was established by £133, the total amount taken being £2,833. An increasing interest - some people think an alarmingly increasing interest - is being taken in most forms of sport nowadays, and particularly Association football, and Saturday's lesson is one that is not likely to go unlearned by the powers that be.'

Crowds along the touchlines, 1936

The Belfast Telegraph were convinced that 'something must be done':

'The IFA, or some of the big clubs, must set about to provide a ground suitable to hold the crowds now attending international matches. The incidents at Windsor Park on Saturday are a lesson that must have taught those responsible that the game has now reached such a height that the grounds of the best clubs in the Irish League will require to be greatly improved if a crowd of such dimensions is to see a match in comfort.

There must have been 50,000 people at this game, and yet only 38,415 paid for admission. When the receipts were made known, it was fully expected all records were broken, as on the occasion when £2,720 was taken over 42,000 paid for admission (the £115 extra on Saturday being accounted for by increased charges). Such, however, was not the case. There must have been ten thousand people who got in free. That is why I say action must be taken to get better grounds. Perhaps the IFA would enter into a conference with the clubs possessing grounds large enough to admit of increasing holding capacity. Certainly after the incidents of last Saturday it is apparent that something must be done, and now is the time to set about dealing with this big problem, and not wait until the next big match is at hand. The fact that Scotland's enthusiasts are coming in such numbers to Ireland for international games [an estimated 5,000 Scots travelled] makes it imperative to improve the holding capacity of the grounds.'

One reader had a particular concern: 'Sir,—With reference to the international match between Ireland and Scotland last Saturday, your correspondent

"Disgusted" has dealt ably with the overcrowding, etc., which took place. My complaint is: Why do so many spectators wear trilby or bowler hats at such a match? At the match (on the 2s enclosure) my view was completely obstructed by four men a little smaller than myself, but with hats on. As a rule I wear a hat myself but always when going to a big match I always discard it for a cap. I think, at least, attention should be drawn to this matter before each international match, as it is lack of thought by those concerned.- Yours, etc., "SPADE-TOWN."

Another man, apparently with a conscience, did pay up after the eventful match:

'The IFA have received 2s conscience money from one who got into Windsor Park on Saturday without paying. There are thousands more who should do the same. Still they are not likely to follow suit. The IFA at their next meeting will likely consider a scheme to deal with the providing of adequate accommodation for spectators at international matches. Clubs with grounds capable of housing such crowds may be asked to co-operate with the association in equipping their grounds so that up to 60,000 spectators can witness matches in comfort, and that a repetition of last Saturday will not take place.'

So it was, then, that the IFA took steps to provide a ground with adequate capacity. Newspapers reported the deliberations of their Council meeting on 31st October 1936, where the IFA President Captain J. M. Wilton advised that the matter had been the subject of discussion by the International Committee, who recommended that the Council should consider the provision either by themselves or by a club of a ground to accommodate from 50,000 to 60,000 people. Such action by the IFA themselves, he pointed out, was not seriously discussed, but it was suggested that one of the clubs might be prepared to enlarge their ground. It should be noted that since 1920, of the 27 home internationals played, 23 had been at Windsor Park.

In response, Mr T. Chambers (Linfield) stated that no one could have foreseen what happened at the international match under discussion. During the last twenty years Linfield had spent over £20,000 on ground improvements. Since the international the Linfield Committee had discussed the position and were prepared to undertake further considerable expenditure with a view to enlarging their ground provided something was done to help them in this respect. He could assure them that so far as the Linfield Club were concerned they would do everything in their power to meet the IFA and the public their demands.

Mr. W. Mullan (Portadown) said he did not agree with Mr. Chambers that no one could have foreseen what happened at Windsor Park. All the stand tickets had been purchased three weeks before the match and that should have been indication to Linfield of what was likely to happen. Linfield failed in their duty and he would object to them getting any rent for the ground.

The matter progressed over the following weeks, and by January 1937 the minute book of the Linfield Committee recorded the Secretary's update on 'the progress made by the Grounds Committee appointed to deal with the proposed additions, as required by the Irish Football Association.'

March 1937 was an eventful month. Quick work by the Belfast Fire Brigade saved the wooden grandstand when an outbreak of fire was discovered. The fire originated in a drying room adjoining the players' quarters underneath the stand. When the brigade arrived smoke was filtering through the floor boards of the stand, giving the impression that the whole structure was ablaze. The outbreak, however, was confined to the drying room, which was burned out. Later, the Linfield Committee signed off on the estimate of £3,377.19.3 from Messrs Harding & Harding, W Miskimmon, H&J Martin, and J&R Thompson Ltd for ground improvements, the work to be completed by September 1937.

In April, the deal between Linfield and the IFA was concluded. A contract was agreed that would see all Ireland's home Internationals played at Windsor Park, for the next 21 years. Linfield agreed to increase the accommodation for spectators to ensure the housing of a crowd of 58,000 and in return the IFA gave a long term contract with a rental for International games for the first seven years of 20 per cent; 15 per cent for the second seven years; and 10 per cent, for the third seven years.

The IFA secretary advised the Council that the Belfast Celtic club had withdrawn from the proposed scheme as they could not get their stand erected owing to the scarcity of steel. The secretary also submitted communications from Mr A. K. Leitch (architect), who had inspected the Windsor Park ground, and said that Linfield could increase their accommodation at the mountain end of the ground by moving their boundary wall back 14 yards.

The proposed accommodation at Windsor Park was – stand seats 4,235, reserved enclosure 12,512, unreserved 35,772 making a total accommodation for 52,519 spectators. Linfield agreed to make passages in the terracing; to make alterations to the stand at the railway side; to erect crush barriers; to arrange for alterations to accommodate 6,000 additional spectators; and to carry out such alterations before October 1937.

Work duly commenced over the summer months. Before the start of the 1937/38 season, Linfield advised spectators 'to show a little consideration, as owing to the alterations at Windsor Park certain parts of the ground have had to be roped off, and if any little inconvenience is caused the Linfield management hope it will be recognised that this is due to the alterations which are of necessity being made.'

The work continued as the season opened, with the target being to have the job finished in time for the Ireland v England match on Saturday, 23rd October.

Works underway on the terracing, 1937

Writing many years later, Linfield fan Billy Smyth recalled 'On the part higher / lowering of the pitch in 1937 that made me 10 years of age, so that was just after Jack Jones was transferred to the Hibs, which nearly broke my heart. My recollection of that particular time is a bit faint. It must have taken time to finish that job. My understanding was they spent a whole summer topping up the pitch with new soil, in addition to extending the terracing all around the ground by a couple of yards by digging lower, as for a couple of years there used to be an old digger on the unreserved [Olympia Drive] side in a big tin hut not far from the unreserved entrance at the front of the ground. On a packed crowd, we as kids used to sit on the roof so we wouldn't get crushed. Then one day the tin roof caved in and we all fell in, and the crowd passed us overhead on to the running track to the St Johns Ambulance.'

The improvements included new arrangements for accessing the ground, as the Belfast Telegraph outlined:

'A sort of dress rehearsal for next Saturday's International took place at Windsor Park on Saturday last [16th October 1937] when Celtic and Linfield met in their League match. Stiles were opened at the back of the stand to admit reserved and unreserved spectators. In fact a test was made of the arrangements and all the officials of the IFA together with the architect, contractor, and clerk of works, were present to see how the crowds came in and how the ground was cleared at the finish. I have the opinion that Windsor Park will be taxed to its utmost next Saturday.'

The match itself was attended by 41,000 spectators, representing gate receipts amounting to £2,660. Ireland lost 1-5 to England.

A report of the Ireland v Scotland international the following year, held on 10th October 1938, gives an insight into the spectacle and occasion of these popular fixtures:

'No Scottish football team has received more enthusiastic and vociferous support than that which defeated Ireland by two clear goals at Windsor Park, Belfast, on Saturday. The city was invaded by about 6,000 Scotsmen on Friday and Saturday morning, and, following the example set by the Welshmen, they immediately proceeded to arm themselves with frying pans, saucepans, and similar utensils with which to emphasise their presence.

Three Burns Laird Line steamers brought the visitors from Glasgow, and throughout Saturday morning Belfast's busy streets were given an extra splash of colour by happy tartan clad crowds. Jaunting cars and buses found them good customers, as also did the restaurants. There was also an additional Steamer service from Stranraer, which arrived at Larne Harbour at 5-50 a.m. The mail and passenger vessels on the same route also carried full complements, and two trains awaited each steamer to convey the passengers to Belfast.

There were over 40,000 spectators in the much improved Windsor Park ground, and it was well that the transport authorities had planned to introduce a service of trams from the city centre at one minute intervals.'

9

1940s

The post World War Two boom

International football matches were suspended for the duration of World War Two, 1939-45. Domestic football competitions were altered too, with the Irish League suspended, though a Regional League was formed.

On Easter Tuesday, 15th April 1941, a crowd had gathered to watch Distillery beat Linfield 3-1 at Windsor Park. Those sports fans were unaware that their city was about to endure what became known as The Easter Raid of the Belfast Blitz. Overhead, a lone Junkers JU-88 plane circled the city centre. Later that evening, between 150-160 bombers left bases in northern France and the Netherlands bound for Belfast. Heinkel HE-111, Junkers JU-88, and Dornier planes made up the attacking force. Elite pathfinder squadron Kampfgruppe 100 lead the first wave, dropping flares to guide following bombers.

Over 900 lives were lost in Belfast that night, the greatest single loss of life in any night raid of the war, outside of London. A later raid, on the 4/5th May, almost completely destroyed Glentoran's home ground, The Oval. It would remain out of use until 1949.

Baseball

In July 1942, 34th Infantry and 1st Armored division all-stars teams were selected to participate in Northern Ireland's first officially recognized baseball game of World War Two. Staged as a part of the Anglo-American Independence Day celebrations, the local government and American military pulled out all the stops to put on a July 4 spectacle.

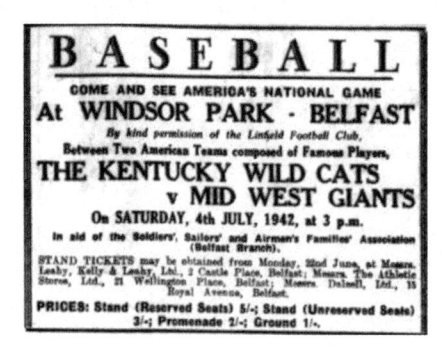

Baseball comes to Belfast, 4th July 1942

The Irish Cup continued, Linfield winning in 1942 and 1945, but losing the 1944 final at Windsor Park to old rivals Belfast Celtic 3-1, in front of a then record crowd for the final of 25,240.

Belfast Celtic taking the field for a wartime cup final via the central tunnel

However, the absence of international matches with large attendances at Windsor Park put any thoughts of further ground improvements, other than general maintenance, on hold.

As the end of the war loomed, particularly after the allies landed in France on D-day, 6th June 1944, some level of normality returned. In September 1944 a representative match between Ireland and a Combined Services team (which included the famous England international Stanley Matthews) took place in front of a new record attendance. The Belfast Telegraph carried reports of the match:

'Ireland v. Combined Services

The march on Windsor this afternoon was one of the biggest in the history of football in Ulster. Before noon many spectators determined to get the best viewpoints had already begun to converge on the ground, and as the time wore on the trickle became a stream, the stream a raging torrent. By bus, tram and train, and on foot they went, thousands upon thousands, taxing the capacity of transport to the last inch. In the city centre it was a case of one way traffic to Windsor and at the peak hour those bound for the ground were boarding trams as far back as Lower Donegall Street, the unbroken line of vehicles ahead of that point being jammed solid with humanity, inside and out.

But the organisation was equal to the load, colossal though it was, and the huge crowds reached their destination in due course. Both the Lisburn and Donegall Roads were black with thousands more who preferred to make the journey on foot.

With nine minutes to go in the match the scores were level at four each, but the Irish defence cracked and the Services added four more goals to win by eight goals to four. More than 50,000 spectators were present—49,875 paid £4,597 for admission – a record attendance for a match in this country. It beats the previous record of 43,000, when Scotland played Ireland on the same ground in February, 1929.'

The return to normality continued after the cessation of hostilities in 1945. Across Britain record crowds, wishing to escape some of the grim realities of the post-war era, were attending games, where admission was cheap for the working man and woman. An unofficial Home International Championship was played, with matches being known as "victory" internationals. Ireland played Scotland at Windsor Park on 2nd February 1946, and the attendance record was smashed again:

'STAND ACCOMMODATION -
Extensions needed at Windsor Park

It seems clear that Linfield will need to proceed with arrangements for further extension to Windsor Park if all who wish to see matches are to be accommodated. There was considerable congestion on Saturday and despite the barriers on the mound at the Bog Meadows end there was a good deal of swaying.

The ground arrangements were handled by the Linfield club, and the fact that there was only one mishap - a gate was broken open and about 1,000 spectators secured free admission - is a great tribute to the club's organisation in handling 4,000 more than on the occasion of the record gate to the September 1944 match. The recorded attendance was 53,000 odd and the cash takings £4,010 plus approximately £900 for the stand. "Spion Kop" has never been so evenly filled, the use of loud speakers with hand microphones being a great asset in directing spectators to open spaces.

A problem for future International matches - should they be all-ticket? The demand for Saturday's match must have been well over 10,000 and the matter will certainly be discussed next season. In the event of it being so decided [that] Windsor Park [be] the International ground for years to come, [it] will require additional crush barriers, gangways, etc.'

There was, however, a tragic consequence to the renewed appetite of the general public to attend "live" games. In England, at Burnden Park on 9th March 1946, an estimated 85,000 spectators turned up for Bolton Wanderers' home Cup match against Stoke City. One end of the ground was packed to capacity and the turnstiles were closed before kick-off, but many thousands more climbed over the closed gates, causing an inevitable crush. 33 people lost their lives, with many more injured. As was the norm in those days, fans paid their entrance fee to the terraces at the gate – matches were not 'all ticket'. This was not an unusual practice – the infamous 1923 'white horse' FA Cup Final at the then new Wembley Stadium was also pay at the gate, and estimates of an overall attendance of 300,000 were made (the ground's official capacity was thought to be around 125,000).

The Burnden Park disaster led to an enquiry and the resultant report came to three conclusions: that the number of spectators present inside the stadium exceeded a safe amount; that the design and shape of the enclosure was at fault; and that the unauthorised entry of supporters was a key factor. The report also made strong recommendations regarding the control of crowds at all football grounds - as a voluntary code, local authorities should inspect grounds with a capacity of 10,000 spectators and agreed safety limits should be in place for grounds of more than 25,000 capacity. Turnstiles should mechanically record spectator numbers and grounds should have internal telephone systems.

The Belfast Telegraph carried the story of the awful disaster in its edition on Monday 11th March 1946. By coincidence, the same page on which the story appeared also had this report of a near-thing in Dublin:

'MANY PEOPLE HURT

A number of boys were injured on Sunday during the Mitre Cup match between Shamrock Rovers and Dundalk at Glenmalure Park, Milltown, Dublin, when, for the second time in less than six weeks, part of a concrete wall surrounding the playing pitch collapsed. About 30 feet of the wall on which the boys were leaning collapsed. The injured were taken to the Meath and Baggot Street Hospital, two suffering from spinal injuries and others from fractures. A large number were treated on the grounds for minor injuries. When the collapse occurred doctor-spectators ran from their places to join players and spectators, who also rushed to the trapped boys. A number of women near the scene fainted.'

Large crowds gathered at Windsor Park on 8th June 1946 as the ground hosted a match between an Irish League select XI and Scottish side Aberdeen as part of the Victory Day celebrations, with proceeds going to local hospitals.

Later that year, in September, a catastrophe similar to that at Blackburn was narrowly avoided at Windsor Park, an event captured on newsreel:

'SPECTATORS' SENSE AVOIDS WINDSOR PARK CALAMITY

An encroachment of spectators on the playing pitch at Windsor Park on Saturday, which might easily have caused a calamity, was happily disposed of. Loud speaker announcements and the common-sense of the crowd, many of whom were forced on to the cinder running track, through no fault of their own, helped to restore order.

The eruption took place on the railway side of the reserved enclosure in which many took up their positions when the gates opened at 12.30. Late-comers finding nowhere to go simply wandered down the cinder track in bewilderment. Warnings by the police proved unavailing. Instead of being able to go back, they were forced forward by the still increasing crowd behind, and the position became very ugly indeed, when many in front of the enclosure, now blotted out from sight of the ground itself, began climbing over the cement wall, while some boys began to throw cinders and others let off squibs. Not knowing where to turn or what to do, they began to squat right up to the touchline.

Crowds spill on to the pitch, 1946

The situation was not eased when those on the mountain-goal side welcomed the example set and rushed right up to the goal line. Three times they advanced and three times they were put back by the police who showed extreme tact and forbearance. The actual scene at three o'clock, when the match was due to start, beggared description. The police did their best, and the referee himself appealed to the crowd to get back, but in vain.

At last a belated call came from the loud speaker: "Attention please! You must get back on the terracing. The game cannot commence until the ground and cinder track are clear." A valiant attempt to obey instructions was made by most of the squatters, but there still was little improvement, owing to the reluctance of those on the terracing to be deprived of positions. Then came another clarion call through the loudspeaker, this time in the form of an ultimatum: "All spectators on the pitch and cinder track must get back on the terracing within three minutes or they will removed from the ground." This had an electrifying effect.

The referee remonstrates with the crowd, 1946

The attendance was easily a record, the official figures being 57,011. The receipts were £5,950. The warm weather and the crush caused some spectators to become faint and they had to be treated by members of the St. John's Ambulance Brigade. Police had charge of crowd control, but congestion at the railway bridge end of the ground was so great that spectators were allowed to go on to the cinder track in order to move freely to less congested parts. People from the area in front of the reserved stand hoping to get better viewpoints, clambered on to the track, men helping women to get over the retaining wall. Then many spectators on the high bank behind the mountain goal, hoping to lie on the green grass around the goal in the sunshine, rushed from their places. Police endeavoured to shepherd them back, and extra men went on the playing enclosure to help, but at the time the game was due to start people were standing five or six deep on the track in front of the reserved stand, blocking the view of others.

There was never any sign of panic, and the crowd remained good-humoured and was thanked by the announcer. During the incident squibs were detonated and again at the end of the game, when sections of the crowd again got on the track, but a Belfast crowd would never mistake these explosions for revolver shots as has been suggested. The spectators, who had sung Land of Hope and Glory to the accompaniment of the band of the Royal Inniskilling Fusiliers, joined in the National Anthem before the start.'

The crowd overspills the Kop, 1946

The huge interest in football prompted Linfield, in 1947, to put forward elaborate plans to further extend the ground's capacity. The plans went through a number of variations over the next few years: ultimately not all the plans came to fruition.

'WINDSOR PARK Plans to accommodate 70,000 spectators

Plans for extending Windsor Park to provide accommodation for 70,000 spectators -17,000 more than the capacity of the ground at present - were outlined by Sir Anthony Babington (president) and Mr. J. O. Mackey (hon. secretary) on behalf of the Linfield club to the Council of the Irish Football Association in Belfast last night. Linfield are seeking an extension of their present agreement with the IFA, whereby they receive a proportion of gate receipts from internationals. This agreement is expected to expire next season when it is estimated that the Association's promise to pay £7,000 to Linfield will have been met. To date the Association have paid £5,160.

The matter has been referred to the Emergency Committee, who are to have consultations with Linfield officials and report to the Council. Sir Anthony Babington said that under the present agreement the club was getting 20 per cent of international gate receipts towards the costs which had been incurred in the past in making the ground adequate for international matches.

The club had two policies before it - a long-term one and a short-term, Sir Anthony explained. Under the short term scheme it was proposed that the stand at the railway end of the ground should be removed, and the wall there, with the stiles, moved back some 18 feet to bring it into line with the houses in Donegall Avenue. There would then be a little more room at that end and a "really respectable entrance" with better turnstiles would be built. The existing stand would be removed and added to the stand at the unreserved side, giving cover there for an additional 6,000 people. In addition, Sir Anthony said, it was proposed that all the exits and entrances would be rearranged in such a way that there would be different sections each with a separate entrance, which would prevent people going through from one section to another.

The short-term plan provided also for the re-terracing of "Spion Kop", which it was eventually intended to raise eight or 10 feet, to provide standing room for another 8,000 or 10,000 people, and which would have its own entrance, separate from all the others. Sir Anthony said the question was whether the proposed work should be undertaken by the Linfield Club on behalf of the IFA. The club had to make certain arrangements of its own, but it did not want to undertake anything too costly until the views of the Association were known. The idea was that the club should obtain long-term extension of the present agreement with the Association and he was instructed to suggest a figure of 15 per cent, of the international gates.

Sir Anthony said that under the club's long-term policy, it was proposed to provide 2,000 additional seats, either at the railway end of the ground or by converting the existing grand stand into double-decker.'

The extension of the contract with the IFA (or rather, a re-negotiated contract, on different terms from that agreed in 1937 and interrupted by the war) was agreed in 1947 at a reduced rental rate of 15% for the next five years.

The detailed plans for expansion were presented to the Linfield Committee at its meeting on 21st October 1947 by the architect, Mr Gibson:

Additional accommodation at the Ground:	
Reserved stand erected at the Railway End	3,500
Space for reserved accommodation under this stand	6,000
Unreserved enclosure and stands	8,500
The total capacity of the ground will therefore be as follows:	
Reserved stands – seating accommodation	8,000
Reserved enclosures	22,500
Unreserved enclosures and stands	41,500
TOTAL CAPACITY	72,000

The plan provided for the removal of the existing stand at the Railway End, and the re-erection of this stand on "Spion Kop".

Whilst no progress was made immediately on the plans for extending the capacity, crowds, however, remained sizeable: the 1948 Irish Cup final between Linfield and Coleraine at Celtic Park attracted 31,000, with the official crowd figure for the Ireland v. England international in October at Windsor Park being 53,629.

The Boxing Day 1948 match between Linfield and Belfast Celtic became infamous due to several unsavoury incidents, the most serious of which saw Celtic player Jimmy Jones physically attacked by a small number of Linfield supporters and thrown into the enclosure where he suffered a broken leg and other injuries. The match itself had immediate ramifications for Linfield and Windsor Park was closed for a number of games scheduled for early 1949, whilst Celtic saw out the rest of their fixtures that season and then withdrew from the Irish League.

A view from the Spion Kop, used in an inquiry into the events of the 1948 Boxing Day Linfield v Belfast Celtic game at which serious crowd disturbances took place. The photo is interesting for showing no fence around the pitch, the poor state of the terracing and also the relatively basic crush barriers. These were later replaced by more sturdy versions

Post-war Windsor Park at an international match. The view is from the railway end and is pre-floodlights and pre-Midgley Park. The photo demonstrates the extent to which the cover at the railway end was not "square" to the pitch dimensions.

In January 1949, Linfield were concerned with attacks on the ground, and the Committee agreed to take all precautions to protect the grandstand. After consultation with the Fire Service and the police, two fire watchers were engaged.

In September 1949 the Belfast News Letter reported the beginning of work on the 1947 proposals:

> 'a start has been made with the cement terracing of "Spion Kop" which is part of the major scheme to increase the capacity from 65,000 to 80,000. Plans have been prepared for adding 16 feet to the railway end of the enclosure and a link fence is being erected on the perimeter wall around the playing pitch.'

10

1950s

Expansion plans, Midgley Park and floodlights

The start of this decade saw the erection of new fencing round the pitch, required as a consequence of the crowd trouble in 1948.

The work on the Kop started in 1949 was not completely satisfactory, and in May 1950 the Linfield Committee engaged architects to assess the viability and cost of increasing the risers to a depth of 4 ½ inches. In September, Linfield priced the costs of additional steps being added to the back of the Kop at £586. In October, however, a decision by the Committee on whether to add more crush barriers was 'left over in the meantime in order that the Committee may see if any undue crush took place on Spion Kop at the International on Saturday'.

That match – Ireland v. England, 7th October 1950 – thankfully passed off without major incident. The Belfast Telegraph revealed that tickets were available in advance for all parts of the ground; and that the better terracing had been added to the Spion Kop:

'The Linfield ground staff had Windsor Park looking a perfect picture with the track covered with red brick dust, and the new terracing at Spion Kop housing a record crowd at that end, while stewards directed occupants of the stand to their seats. Letters of congratulation have reached me on the marshalling of the crowd by the Royal Ulster Constabulary, both on entering and more particularly on their leaving the ground. Last, but certainly by no means least, that grand band of St. John Ambulance Corps, who efficiently handled a number of minor casualties amongst the spectators from faintness. An interested spectator at the match was Jimmy Jones, of Fulham, who was looking extremely fit and showed no traces of any effects of that broken leg.'

The track around the pitch was a terracotta compound, using material similar to that used in the making of hard lawn tennis courts, the cost of the work being £400. The job was not completed until a few hours before the international.

The plans for a new stand at the railway end – first mooted as part of the 1947 proposals – were presented to the Linfield Committee at their meeting

Various newsreel footage was taken of international and representative matches from the 1950's onwards, all of which give good views of the ground as it then was. These newsreel films were shot from a platform erected over a new player's tunnel erected at the south-west corner between the grand stand and the Kop, as seen in this photo from 1954

in December 1950. The plan was for seating of 3,500 and cover underneath for 3,000, at a cost of around £40,000. The pavilion was to be moved to this end from under the grand stand, and the existing pavilion area converted to an indoor training track.

Despite the planning and by now four year old proposals, progress on extending the capacity was slow. More general improvements were needed, and in September 1951 the Linfield committee agreed to scale back on the plans for economic reasons:

> 'The ground committee intimated that they would like to have the terracing underneath the reserved stand completed in concrete'.

> 'The architects, Gibson & Taylor, submitted a plan showing the front wall and a new stand with seating accommodation for approximately 2,200. Mr Gibson stated they had taken into consideration the erection of an additional deck to the present stand and rounding off the corners of the existing stand, but that neither of these would be an economic proposition. They had, therefore, decided, on the grounds of economy, to continue the present rake at the railway end, and build a single decker stand which would take the place of the original plan contemplated some years ago and by doing so there would be a considerable reduction in the cost of the work.

> The scheme also provides for the existing stand at the railway end being reconstructed at Spion Kop. The first stage of the work would commence at the Balmoral end, providing for 70 - 90 yards of new entrances, turn stiles, enclosures etc, and which is estimated to cost

£3,000. It was resolved that the first stage of the work be proceeded with.'

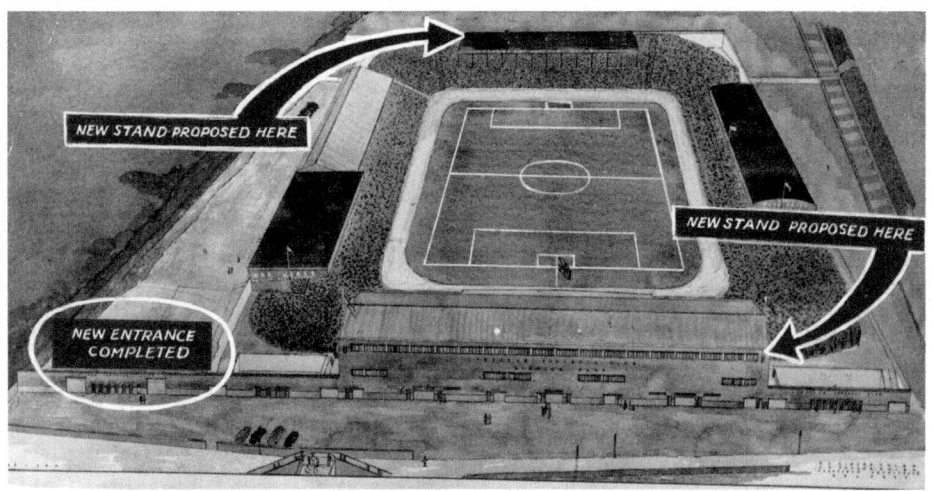

A sketch showing the completed work at the entrance, and the proposals for new stands at the railway end and Spion Kop – neither of which were progressed

In October 1951 the Ireland v. Scotland match was made an all-ticket affair. Fifty-eight thousand tickets were printed in anticipation of a new ground record.

Windsor Park in the post-war years, with notable features (clockwise):

Footbridge bottom right (1913)
Covered enclosure at the railway end (the roof from 1907, moved here in 1930)
Balmoral Stand (with flat roof, 1929)
Grandstand (as designed by Leitch, 1930)
Spion Kop (the land behind which would become Midgley Park in 1955)
Covered unreserved enclosure ("Olympia"), roof dating from 1909

Financial worries were concerning the Linfield Committee in April 1952. The team had just finished its worst season, winning no major trophies and finishing 10th out of 12 in the Irish League. Economies had to be made, and the Committee minutes reported: 'Further extensions and new works to be discontinued, except repairs which were absolutely essential'.

The contract with the IFA to host internationals was renewed in May 1952 for five years, with Linfield accepting reduced terms of 12.5% of the gross gates for the English and Scottish matches, and 10% of the gross gate for all other matches under the IFA's control.

In October 1952 the Ireland v. England home international match saw an end to the traditional transportation to Windsor Park:

'LAST BIG DAY FOR THE TRAMS

Since the beginning of this century trams have conveyed countless thousands of fans from the city centre to Windsor Park for International matches, representative games and the many clashes in which the "Blues" have been engaged. But the era of the tram is passing, and today was the last "big day" when trams with their clanging bells carried the crowds. Next month, it everything goes according to schedule, buses will replace trams on the Lisburn Road, and yet another route will have passed over to more modern methods of travel.

Trams to-day did not go out unnoticed. Line after line moved slowly to Windsor Park with the same crowds conveyed in the same way, on the upper deck, the lower deck, the platform and on the "bumper." An official of Belfast Corporation Transport Department said crowds were moving to the ground from shortly after noon. The Ulster Transport Authority augmented their rail and bus services from the country. The Great Northern Railway ran special trains from several areas and attached extra carriages to the ordinary trains. Day excursionists from Dublin travelled by the morning services, which were strengthened, and late trains were put on to the Warrenpoint and Enniskillen directions'.

In 1954, demonstrating that Windsor Park still hosted a range of sports other than football, the Linfield Committee gave permission for the ground to be used for a competition held by the Ulster Archery Association. The ground also hosted a rugby league exhibition game, between Warrington and Halifax, in May 1954.

That season's Irish Cup final between Glentoran and Derry City was hosted at Windsor Park, the first match being drawn in front of an attendance of over 35,000. However the first of two midweek replayed finals caused crowd access problems. A stampede occurred outside the reserved enclosure. The Belfast Telegraph set out the circumstances:

'(1) No one anticipated an over 30,000 attendance, including the thousands of spectators who reached the ground half an hour or less before kick-off. The total stiles open (24) therefore averaged 1,200 or, say, 200 per hour or over three every minute. There are three doors in front of the reserved enclosure— THESE ARE NOT STILES and obviously were not open.

(2) The City Transport Authorities are unable to provide for an international attendance service at night peak hour.

(3) Repairs to the railway bridge on the Donegall Road caused traffic to be diverted to the Lisburn Road, adding to the bottle-neck over the bridge at Windsor Park.

(4) When the Stand stiles were closed (about 7 o'clock) this caused a rush from these to the reserved enclosures, and the queues were broken, a panic following.

(5) The numbers quoted as unable to obtain admission have been generally wildly exaggerated, but there is no method of checking the figures. A reasonable estimate puts the figure at under 2,000.

For to-night's game [the second replay] the co-operation of all concerned is requested. First, the stand has been booked, and overcrowding will not, therefore, occur. Police will regulate the queues outside the ground. Spectators are reminded of the four stiles at the Bog Meadows end leading to Spion Kop, where there was no rush. All should endeavour to reach the ground at the very earliest possible time. Most important is that the hour of kick-off has been brought forward 15 minutes which will obviously cause an even greater congestion, unless spectators make sure of getting to the ground well before that hour.'

Crowd problems of a different kind were evident in October 1954, with reports of casualties at a home international game:

'St. John Ambulance Brigade dealt with 124 cases at the Ireland v. England International at Windsor Park on Saturday, a Brigade official stated yesterday. Of these two were sent to hospital for further treatment and the rest, mainly fainting cases, were dealt with on the field. Many of the fainting cases were due to inadequate meals before the match.'

Also that month, the press reported that the plans to expand the ground's capacity, first proposed in 1947, though with a few adjustments, were yet again back on:

'BIG EXTENSION SCHEME PASSED BY CORPORATION

Windsor Park is to be enlarged to hold 81,000 spectators, with seating accommodation for almost 8,000. Work is to commence on January 1 and it is hoped to have it completed for the Ireland v. Scotland international in October, 1955. The front of the present reserved enclosure stand is to be taken forward 27 feet, and a new stand is to be built with 3,000 – 4,000 tip-up seats installed. The present covering will be taken to the Spion Kop end, and re-erected there, thus providing covered accommodation on all four sides of the pitch. On the North side of Spion Kop, three and a half acres of land have been purchased, on which a pitch for the third eleven of the club will be made. On international days, this pitch will be used as a car park to accommodate 1,200 cars. Entrances will be arranged for admission to the stands and enclosures from this park. All unreserved stiles will be moved to the East side of the ground on Olympia Drive, with 12 stiles at each end of the enclosure.

Underneath the new stand a gymnasium, with billiards room, first aid room, and an indoor training track, in addition to facilities for News Reel pictures, will be built. On the new three and a half acres it is intended to later erect 10 or 12 houses for letting to players of the club. The total estimated cost of the project is £40,000, and the plans prepared by the architects Messrs. Gibson & Taylor have already been passed by the Belfast Corporation'.

Linfield remained cautious about committing to all aspects of the proposed extension scheme, and in 1955 the proposals had been further amended to a more modest new stand at the railway end, a new ground for the third eleven, plus a car park for about 1,000 cars at the Spion Kop end. The cost was estimated at £45,000, and in 1955 Linfield purchased the land adjacent to the Kop.

The land behind Spion Kop, purchased for the provision of a training pitch and car park

In the event, no changes were made to the existing accommodation, although the Linfield match day programme of the time contained an artist's impression of the proposals:

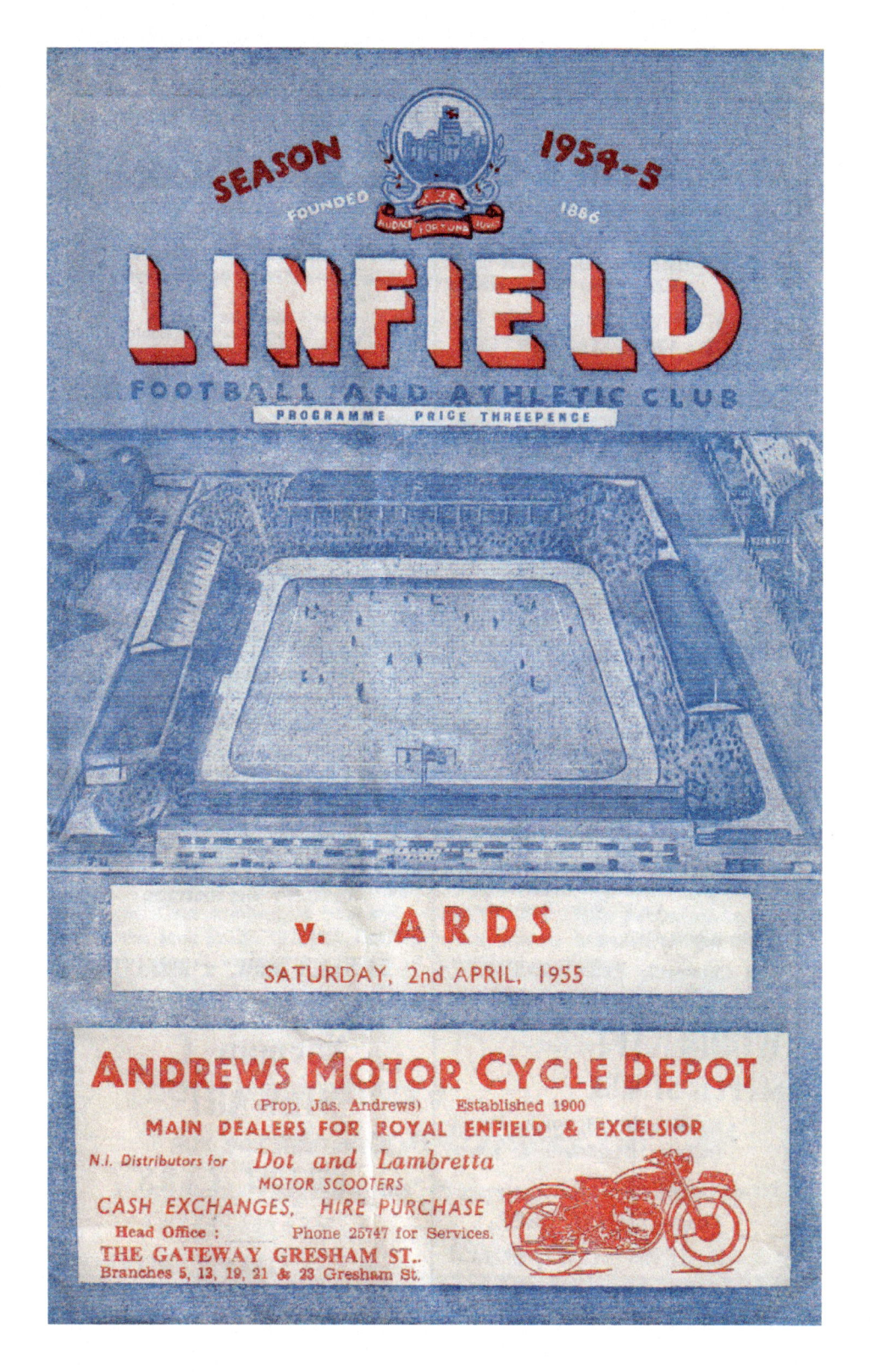

As perhaps a sign of the times, and the increasing reliance on motor vehicles for transport rather than trams and trains, Linfield announced at the start of the 1955/56 season that new car-parking arrangements were available at Ebor Drive (rear of Spion Kop), at 1 shilling per car, with 'entrance from new car park to grandstand provided.'

The new pitch at the rear of the Spion Kop was opened on 22nd October 1955 before the Linfield Swifts v. Newry Town match. In its early incarnation it was mostly surfaced with cinder, with the hope being it would be in 'full grass' the following season. The new pitch was named Midgley Park in honour of Harry Midgley MP, the Linfield Chairman.

Floodlights

The early 1950's saw floodlights installed in most of the large stadia across the United Kingdom. Before 1950 the English Football Association would not sanction games held under lights. Clubs everywhere could see the benefit of being able to stage matches at night time as well as maintaining the traditional 3.00pm kick off time during the dark winter months.

In 1951 Linfield trialled a new floodlighting system, officially opened by the Lord Mayor of Belfast. The floodlighting consisted of six lamps, each of 1,500 watts shining from the grandstand. It was intended to add 12 lamps on the grandstand, 12 on the terraces and a bank of 2 lights shining from each corner of the ground, but the scheme, estimated to cost around £6,000, was not completed.

Players from Linfield Rangers had the honour of playing the first match – a five-a-side – on the newly floodlit pitch, and it was reported that 'the players and the white ball were easily visible from the stand'.

In 1953, four Belfast clubs agreed to play in a 'floodlight league', utilising the new lights installed at Distillery's Grosvenor Park.

Planning for a complete system began in earnest in 1955 with club officials studying the various systems used elsewhere, being particularly impressed with the lights installed at Easter Road, Edinburgh, home of Hibernian.

Tenders were issued in early 1956 with the Edinburgh firm of Millar and Stables winning the contract. Installation took around nine weeks over the summer months. Four 100-foot pylons were erected, with 30 lamps of varying types on each pylon—all separately focused to provide a non-glare, shadowless system, technically known as drench lighting.

WINDSOR PARK - A History of the Home of Linfield FC & Northern Ireland

New floodlights being built on Spion Kop, 1956

Laying of electricity cables to the new floodlight pylons

After testing, including in fog conditions, the lights were officially switched on by Lord Brookeborough, the Northern Ireland Prime Minister, on 10th October 1956. The estimated cost of the lighting was £15,000. Linfield's visitors for the occasion were Newcastle United, and on the same evening new press room facilities were opened. The occasion was a great success, as Malcolm Brodie wrote in the Belfast Telegraph:

'Football has arrived in Northern Ireland. That was how I felt when Linfield and Newcastle United walked out on to the floodlit Windsor Park pitch before a crowd of 30,000 last night, shortly after Lord Brookeborough had switched on the 115,000 watt "drench lighting" system. Linfield had lifted the game out of the parochial. And I write that without detracting from the glory of Distillery, to whom falls the honour of being the pioneers of floodlit football in Ireland.

They have provided us with many entertaining games and no doubt will do so in the future. Their progressiveness, too, was something to be admired. But even the most ardent Whites fan will, I think, give full credit to Linfield on the introduction of one of the best floodlighting systems in Europe.

There were one or two shaded patches which should be eliminated with slight re-focusing. No filters however were erected on the lamps as a precaution against fog. 'There are no such things as filters on floodlights' an official of the General Electric Company said to-day.

Once these lamps are re-focussed then Windsor will be ready for a great future under this pylon radiance which is gradually revolutionising our national game. Linfield have thought big on this project. And in the future, too, they intend to do the same.

Not for them any third-rate fixtures under the lights. Matches must be competitive - expect a few Irish League tussles to be arranged - or the opposing teams exceptionally attractive. For instance, efforts are being made to induce Glasgow Rangers, Hibs and a number of Continental sides while there are proposals to seek entry into the unofficial British Floodlit League or the European Cup.

A new Press Room was officially opened last night, too, by Mr. HC Midgley, Minister of Education and Linfield chairman. This has cubicles for almost 25 for the transmission of pictures by tele-photo and radio. On the Press benches in the stand, lights have been fitted at each reporter's seat, another amenity which makes Windsor unsurpassed as a stadium in Ireland.'

WINDSOR PARK - A History of the Home of Linfield FC & Northern Ireland

The view from the press box circa late 1960s

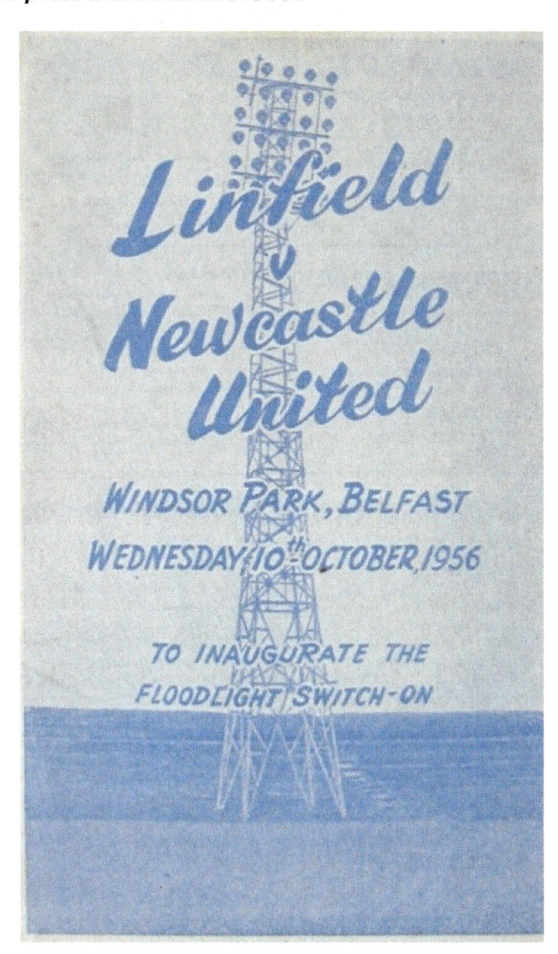

Programme cover for opening of the new floodlights

The visitors featured the England international Jackie Milburn, who impressed the Linfield Committee so much that they persuaded him to join the club as player-coach the following year.

Linfield began using the new lights for domestic games that season, and the new facility also allowed a floodlit rugby union match to be played, when the Vigilantes met the Wolfhounds in December 1956, a venture sponsored by the Collegians, Instonians and Malone clubs in aid of their ground funds. In August 1957, over 1,000 pipers and drummers gathered under the lights for a massed pipe band event.

The first international match under the new floodlights was on 23rd October 1957 when Northern Ireland played Romania in a B international: 'Linfield's magnificent, new-fangled floodlights came lancing through the darkness. Northern Ireland's first illuminated international was on. And some ultra-cautious souls actually donned dark glasses to counter such incredible brightness.'

Earlier that year, in April 1957, a fire broke out during the Ireland v Wales international, in circumstances ominously prescient to events in Bradford in 1985. The News Letter carried the report of the incident:

> 'Firemen and not footballers created most of the excitement last night at Windsor Park, where Ireland and Wales played a goalless draw in one of the poorest internationals by teams of the two countries. Just as the game was about to end and bring relief to the boredom, fire broke out in the top corner of the stand at the "Spion Kop" end of the ground. Spectators were filing out of their seats quietly when the alarm was raised. Fire extinguishers and water were applied to smouldering wood. The prompt action confined the damage to a few boards and there was no panic.
>
> As a precautionary measure the Fire Brigade was summoned. Two machines were despatched from the Lisburn Road station and they had to pass their way through the crowd leaving the ground. One jet was used, but only to make certain that the fire was out.
>
> It is believed to have been caused by a lighted cigarette end, and it was fortunate that the discovery was made while the ground was occupied, otherwise the stand might have been severely damaged. There was a strong wind blowing to fan the flames had they got a grip on the building, which has wood flooring and seats.'

During the 1957/58 season the contract with the IFA for the use of the ground was renewed for a further fixed term.

In January 1958 the first match at Windsor Park to be 'live' televised was broadcast across the UK. Previously some home internationals had been recorded for television highlights packages. The Belfast Telegraph provided the details of the operation:

'Millions of people will be able to watch the Ireland-Italy postponed World Cup tie at Windsor Park, Belfast next Wednesday on television. All except the opening ten minutes of the game will be televised "live" by the BBC to all parts of the United Kingdom and, through the Eurovision link, to Italy and Belgium. This is the first occasion that a soccer match has been televised direct from Ireland. Hitherto, only films have been shot for screening that evening or at a later date. A BBC spokesman said in London to-day that a substantial fee had been paid for the television rights of the game. "The interest in this match is phenomenal," he added. Meanwhile, in Belfast Mr. J. A. Robinson, the Publicity Officer of the BBC announced that the transmission would commence at 2.25pm and last until the end of the game. Kenneth Wolstenholme will be the commentator. Already the stand tickets have been allocated and the sale on the enclosure and ground tickets has been quite brisk.

Assured, therefore, of financial success, the Irish F.A. have acted in the best interests of the public in agreeing to the "live" broadcast. It is a decision which all will applaud. For the BBC, too, it is a "scoop" and a technical triumph. Four cameras will be operated at Windsor Park—three in a fixed position, while the fourth will be a small mobile hand camera with the transmitter on the cameraman's back. He can "shoot" from any part of the stadium. Getting the picture from Windsor Park into the BBC channel is quite a complex operation. A mobile control room and transmitter will be set up in the car park at the ground and the producer will be operating in this. From this point the picture will be sent to Divis. Two mobile transmitters in Scotland will then relay it to Kirk o' Shotts, the main Scottish transmitter, for injection into the national network. Approximately how many will see the game on the screen? I put that question to a BBC official to-day but he was unable to give an assessment. "For the Manchester United-Aston Villa Cup final last May, there was a viewing public of 12,000,000 in the United Kingdom alone." he said.'

Two of the cameras were positioned within the grand stand with a third on a temporary structure at the back of the Kop.

The temporary camera position on the Kop

In May 1959, the ground entertained visitors from the USA - the famous Harlem Globetrotters basketball team.

'Globetrotters use Australian floor at Windsor Park

One of the highlights of the year in the world of sport and entertainment will be the visit of the world famous Harlem Globetrotters to Belfast on May 30th. Local arrangements are being made by the Ulster Basketball Council, who announce that all is ready for the big occasion. The event will be staged in Windsor Park, where there will be accommodation for 4,000 seated and 6,000 standing at each of the two shows. Biggest worry was the provision of a playing surface, but this has been solved by the promise of a portable wooden floor being imported specially by the Globetrotters from Australia. Wet or dry the show must go on and with the large grandstand at Windsor offering cover for spectators the weather is not of very great importance. School children are being admitted to the 3 pm show at half price. For "the adults only" performance at 7.15 p.m. ticket sales have been astonishing - a large proportion of the choice seats having been already booked during their first week of sales. This is not only a sportsman's show: it is a show for the family, which combines amazing skill with fun and frolic.'

In September 1959 Linfield played their first competitive European match, facing Swedish side IFK Goteborg at home in the first of a two-legged tie in the preliminary round of the European Cup. Inspired by player-manager Jackie Milburn, Linfield won 2-1 with Milburn scoring both goals under the lights in front of a huge attendance. Malcolm Brodie noted in the Belfast Telegraph:

> 'What was the strength of last night's crowd at Windsor Park? Some say it would have been impossible to get another 20,000 into the ground while others contend that the spectators were "lightly packed" and only numbered 30,000. I asked an official of the Linfield club today. Said he: 'Judging from our returns, there must have been between 40,000 and 42,000 in the ground last night.'

Later that year part of the covering over the unreserved terracing was destroyed:

> 'At the height of the storm a section of the unreserved stand at Windsor Park, Belfast, was torn from its stanchions and thrown more than 200 feet in the air crashing on the rooftops on both sides of nearby Olympia Drive. Today huge gaping holes in the roofs and shattered chimneys told the story of the night before. Only one person was on the street when the roof took off. 12 year old Jackie Johnston was on his way to a fish and chip shop at the time. "It came sailing through the air like an aeroplane" he told his parents, "I ran for my life".'

11

1960s

Reducing the capacity

There were some minor changes in the 1960s and one significant one – the decision to place seats under the railway end roof. This had the effect of reducing the capacity of the ground from circa 60,000 to around 48,600.

Linfield supporters played their part in necessary repairs and general ground maintenance. In 1961, the Linfield Supporters' Development Organisation announced that the first priority in their programme of ground improvements at Windsor Park was the re-surfacing of the front of the ground. The Organisation had spent £2,000 in the previous year on immediate repairs – resurfacing terracing, structural repairs to the ground, installation of showers and baths for the players. The bulk of the cash obtained by the Development Organisation came from pools and grants, gifts etc from the various Linfield supporters' clubs.

Surfacing the forecourt at the railway end, 1961

Earlier that year an altogether different event was held at Windsor Park, when 50,000 people gathered to hear the American evangelist Dr Billy Graham preach. As the Belfast Telegraph described it 'the terraces were packed tight as for any soccer international, and the pitch itself ringed with rows of seats. But instead of dunchers and dungarees this was a dress occasion, for the women and menfolk alike. Belfast likes to dress up for church, and whether it is a tin tabernacle or a football stadium, out comes the Sunday suit and lacy white hat'.

Billy Graham crusade June 1961

In 1962, more repairs were reported, including the re-surfacing of the entrance behind the main stand, and improvements to the floodlighting system, with the lights being re-focused and the entire system re-wired.

In 1963 the Harlem Globetrotters paid their second visit to Windsor Park:

The occasion was billed as 'The Harlem Globetrotters plus 9 Sensational Variety Acts. Belfast August 8th. Also at Recreation Grounds Portrush Friday night'.

In September, Windsor Park hosted the European Cup match between Distillery and the Portuguese champions Benfica, the match being switched from Distillery's Grosvenor Park ground to allow for the expected large attendance – Benfica had reached the final of the competition at Wembley four months earlier. 20,000 turned up to see Distillery, boosted by the inclusion of former Preston North End star and England international Tom Finney, who at 41 years of age had been coaxed out of retirement for the occasion. The game finished 3-3. Finney didn't score for Distillery, who took the lead on three occasions, Benfica's Eusebio scoring the third equaliser.

Minor improvements continued in the 1964 close season to the stands, terraces and pitch, and the secretary's office was refurbished. An article in the Belfast Telegraph in 1965 gave an indication of other costs to Linfield relating to the ground. It reported discussions of a committee of the Londonderry Corporation on a proposal to improve the Brandywell, home ground of Derry City: 'the committee was told that the rates on certain football grounds in Belfast were: - Windsor Park £1,550; The Oval £960; Grosvenor Park £530; Cliftonville £600; Seaview £350'.

Linfield's poor form that season led to a slump in attendances, and an April match against Bangor attracted fewer than 2,000 people. The contract with the IFA to host internationals was due to expire in July 1966, and Glentoran, Linfield's great east Belfast rivals, made a pitch to win the contract. The Glens had played at their ground, The Oval, since 1903, and had previously staged internationals, representative games and Irish Cup finals. Glentoran's use of the ground was originally on a long-term lease from the Dixon family, but that changed in January 1960 when the club bought the ground outright, and unveiled plans to expand the capacity to around 70,000. As part of the plan, floodlights had been installed in 1964.

In January 1966, Glentoran secretary Billy Ferguson was quoted as saying 'We've large-scale plans ready and feel our amenities are sufficient now for these big games', as the club unveiled plans for the provision of 1,100 additional seats beneath the main stand at The Oval, and 3,500 seats in the unreserved stand. Terracing was to be built up, car park arrangements improved, and an electric scoreboard installed. There was also talk of building a bridge over the adjacent railway line.

In response, Linfield announced plans to provide a new stand at the railway end of Windsor Park and a replacement for the 'old' part of the grand stand. The IFA Finance Committee deferred a decision at their March 1966 meeting and the Belfast Telegraph speculated that some thought was given to sharing the contract with both grounds. In August, Linfield pressed ahead with their plan and the railway end covering was converted to seating.

The seated area of the Railway Stand consisted of six rows of bench seating, numbered 1 – 110. The seated area used approximately a third of the span of the roof, leaving the remaining two thirds as "dead" storage space. The seats did not extend the full length of the roof, which overhung remaining terracing at the south-east corner. This end roofing was removed sometime later, as various later photographs show the floodlight pylon originally in front of the roof whilst latterly the pylon stands in front of free space.

Eventually, in October 1966, the IFA made their decision on which ground should host future international games, agreeing a ten-year contract with Linfield with a 12% ground rent, and an option to extend for a further

Railway Stand being prepared for new seating

five years. Glentoran Director, Paddy Hunt, described it as 'absolutely scandalous', adding 'I felt we had an unbeatable case. We spent over £30,000 on the Oval in the last couple of years. What's the use of throwing more money into improving amenities in view of this?' Oval secretary Billy Ferguson was just as forthright: 'they can keep their internationals' he said. 'If we bring across top class continental clubs – and we have the means to do this – then we will get enough revenue to compensate for the loss of these big games'.

Underneath the Railway Stand roof

The Ireland v. England match on 22nd October 1966 saw a reduced capacity due to the recently installed seating area at the railway end. The attendance was recorded as 47,897.

This was England's first match since winning the World Cup that summer, and captain Bobby Moore carried the Jules Rimet trophy as the teams entered the pitch. It was a memorable match for a different reason for Linfield winger Billy Ferguson, who was sent off with 5 minutes remaining for a nasty challenge on Alan Ball.

The following year, a crowd of 13,500 at a Linfield v Glentoran match were kept informed of the outcome of the television series 'The Fugitive' as the long screen chase of Dr. Richard Kimble entered its final stages, with the result announced over the loudspeakers.

In 1968 a new official entrance at the rear of the grand stand, and renovated dressing rooms were built. Also in the late 1960's, a more permanent television platform was built on top of the main grandstand.

WINDSOR PARK - A History of the Home of Linfield FC & Northern Ireland

Windsor Park late 1960's, with the new seats installed in the Railway Stand

The new entrance 1968

12

1970s

Troubled times

Belfast, and Northern Ireland, suffered from widespread disruption throughout the 1970s – "The Troubles" had broken out in 1969 when sectarian tensions spilled over into street violence. As parts of Belfast became "no-go" areas, crowds attending football matches dwindled, and night matches became the exception. One famous old Belfast club, Distillery, were forced to leave their Grosvenor Park ground, and another club, Derry City, left the Irish League altogether after attacks on a visiting team's bus led other clubs to refuse to travel to Derry's Brandywell ground. Windsor Park was also a target for terrorists on a few occasions.

Northern Irish teams did not enter the European club competitions in 1972 due to the security situation, and 'home' international games were not able to be hosted in Belfast from 1971 to 1975, depriving Linfield of anticipated income. International games were switched to various grounds in England, including Goodison Park (Liverpool), Boothferry Park (Hull), Highfield Road (Coventry), Hillsborough (Sheffield) and Craven Cottage (London).

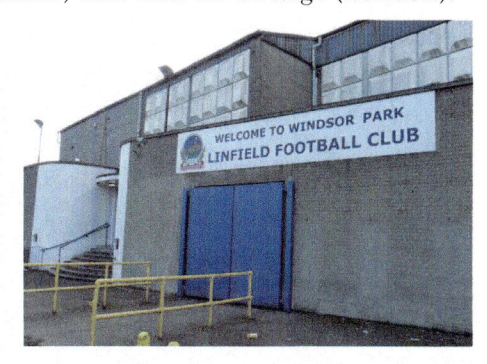

The Viewing Lounge

At Windsor Park, further low level remedial and maintenance work continued to be carried out despite the scarcity of resources. Perhaps to mitigate that, Linfield opened a new Social Club in 1970. Situated at the corner between the Railway and 'Balmoral' stands, it was designed to be a lucrative source of income. On match days, the upper floor allowed supporters to watch the action from a heated Viewing Lounge, with full bar facilities. Outside of football matches, the Club hosted dances, cabaret and snooker games. The Club was extended later in the decade.

The Troubles had other impacts. When Linfield drew Manchester City in the European Cup-Winners' Cup in September 1970 (City were the holders having won the final in April that year), the home game at Windsor Park was ordered by the police to kick off at 6.45pm, in order that the expected large crowd could leave the match in relative daylight. Nevertheless, Linfield fans turned out in large numbers to see the team record a 2-1 victory but exit the tournament on the away goals rule having lost the first leg 1-0 in Manchester. The match was watched by an attendance of close on 25,000 and gate receipts were around £7,000, a European record for the club.

In 1972 the club announced plans to install floodlights at Midgley Park, at which a small covered stand had been added. In April that year, the railway end of the main ground suffered damage as a result of a terrorist attack:

'A bomb inside a parked van damaged the entrance to Windsor Park football ground this morning and shattered windows in the social club and surrounding houses. Two people were treated for shock in the blast which happened shortly before noon but some of the staff at the ground had a lucky escape. Mrs. Christina Purvis, of Tate's Avenue, who was cleaning in the social centre, said she and a groundsman looked inside the van shortly before the bomb went off. Mrs. Purvis, still shaken from her experience, said: "We looked in and saw a box and I said 'don't go near it, come away'. We had just come back into the social centre when it went off. There were four children here when the windows came in. These people don't care what they do".

And a member of the club, Mr. Walter Davidson, said he had chased some boys who were playing football in the open ground where the van exploded shortly before the blast. The people in the ground said they received no

A view of the damage caused in the 1972 bomb attack

warning of the explosion. An anonymous caller earlier told police that a bomb had been planted in "a Linfield social club" of which there are several in different parts of the city. The blast tore down the wall at the rear of the stand at the east end of the ground where the turnstiles are situated. Windows in the club's new social centre were broken but no structural damage was done and it is not thought that the stand itself was severely damaged.'

On Friday 21st July 1972 at least twenty bombs planted by the IRA exploded across Belfast in the space of eighty minutes, most within a half hour period. The day became known as 'Bloody Friday' as there were scores of civilians injured, and nine people killed in the attacks. The footbridge at Windsor Park was one of the terrorist targets; at 2.09pm a bomb estimated at 30 pounds of explosive was detonated on it.

Although The Troubles continued to disrupt everyday life, international football did return to Windsor Park in 1975. The Welsh FA announced that they would fulfil the Home International fixture in Belfast in May; the English FA soon followed. Before those games, in April, Windsor Park hosted its first international in four years, Northern Ireland beating Yugoslavia 1-0, with the goal scored by former Linfield player Bryan Hamilton. The crowd was estimated at 28,000.

The return of international games highlighted the heavy costs to Linfield of maintaining the stadium in an acceptable condition, particularly at a time when income from Linfield's home games had diminished as crowds continued to dwindle. In 1977, Malcolm Brodie reported in the Belfast Telegraph that other clubs were unhappy about the prospect of direct government aid to assist with ground improvements:

'Glentoran's board of directors have agreed to circularise all Irish League clubs for round table talks on the necessity for Government money allocated to football, to be distributed equally. Last week it was announced that the Government would give 50% grant aid up to a maximum of £40,000 for the improvement of Windsor Park, Belfast's international stadium and Linfield's headquarters. "This is no attack on Linfield, but it is entirely unfair that one club should be dealt with specifically while the others are left more or less out in the cold wondering if anything can be done for them" said Glentoran director Harry McNeely. I put it to Mr. McNeely that the money had been allocated not to Linfield but to the Irish FA for international amenities. "Windsor is not the national stadium." he replied. "It belongs to Linfield who have only a five-year agreement with the IFA. What happens when this expires and say the contract is not renewed? Does it mean that £40,000 of Government money is going into something over which the Irish FA might eventually have no control," he said.'

A side view of the unreserved side, late 1970s

Linfield v Moscow Dynamo match programme 20 November 1978

An aerial shot from the 1970's (note the Viewing Lounge has not yet been extended)

Despite the concerns of others, the government did provide funding for the upgrading of the Windsor Park floodlights. In November 1978 Linfield invited Moscow Dynamo to celebrate the opening of the £100,000 floodlighting system, switched on by Roy Mason MP, then Secretary of State for Northern Ireland.

The work was carried out by Weir and McQuiston of York Road, Belfast. 9,000 fans turned out on a wet wintry evening as the Blues lost 4-0.

The routine of continual maintenance of the aging ground continued. In 1979 Linfield announced that there were still a lot of improvements needed at the ground, including new turnstiles and fencing around the pitch, and resurfacing at the front of the ground to improve access for motorists and pedestrians coming to matches.

Linfield estimated this first stage of improvements as costing approximately £100,000; further stages of a development programme were estimated to cost in the region of £3/4 million.

In many ways, Windsor Park in the 1970s could claim similarities with many of the grounds of English First Division clubs – a capacity of around 48,000, with over 5,000 seats, and both covered and open terracing put it on a par with the grounds of Derby County and Leeds United (both First Division championship winners in the decade), Newcastle United and Chelsea. That was all to change in the next 10-15 years

13

1980s

A new stand for Windsor

The 1980s were to see the end of the "classic" Windsor Park and the first moves towards its re-design as a modern stadium. The decade also saw tragic events elsewhere, at Bradford, Brussels and Sheffield, which would have an impact on the safety and design of sports grounds across the UK.

Trouble of another kind – between rival fans as Linfield played a European tie away to Republic of Ireland side Dundalk – led to a UEFA ban on 'home' European fixtures anywhere within the UK for two seasons, and Linfield played their 'home' fixtures in 1979 and 1980 at the HFC Stadium, Haarlem.

In a more positive sign of an incremental return to normality, Linfield hosted Manchester United in a hastily arranged friendly in February 1981. The English club had been unable to train and play due to a severe winter in England and their full first team was given a scare in the match before clinching a narrow 1-0 victory. Over 30,000 fans packed into the ground. Friendlies against Everton, Tottenham Hotspur, Rangers and the East Germany national side were to follow.

In terms of structural changes, the decade saw a low-key start, with Linfield announcing 610 new tip-up seats in the main grandstand at Windsor Park, bringing the total to 1,100. These were offered to Linfield season ticket holders on payment of an extra £2 on top of their annual subscription of £18. These new tip-up seats replaced the original benches in Section D of the grandstand, the area directly in front of the press box.

Old bench seats in Section D of the grand stand, in front of the press box

As in the early 1970's, The Troubles impacted on the Home Internationals, with the scheduled home games against England and Wales in May 1981 cancelled due to tensions on the streets arising from the death of IRA hunger striker Bobby Sands.

Later that year, however, in November, the ground was filled to the brim when an estimated 40,000 fans cheered Northern Ireland's 1-0 win over Israel which clinched qualification to the 1982 World Cup finals. Buoyed by that success, and the financial opportunities that qualification would provide, the IFA commissioned a feasibility study in March 1982 to assess the replacement of the unreserved terracing at Olympia Drive with a new grandstand capable of seating 6,000 – 7,000 spectators.

Before plans could be advanced, the unreserved stand roof went up in flames, on April 6th 1982. Linfield had defeated Glentoran 1-0 in a County Antrim Shield tie earlier that evening. The fire was spotted by a supporter in the Social Club and the Fire Brigade were quickly summoned but the first of their engines pulled into the main entrance at the grandstand side of the ground only to be re-directed to the unreserved. One or two people had already rushed across the pitch armed with fire extinguishers, but the blaze was much more serious than it first seemed. Eventually the firemen were able to train their hoses on the blaze which was spreading along the roof, parts of which caved in.

The extent of the damage to the unreserved cover is revealed

The remaining roof was demolished during the summer of 1982, and the plans to build a new, 6,800 seated stand on the site gathered pace. The preparation of drawings, contract and tender documents was completed in 20 weeks with a six-week tender and acceptance period. The contract was awarded to Banbridge firm JMJ Contractors for the sum of £1,688,000 so that work could commence in 1983. The uncovered terrace was to remain open for Linfield and Northern Ireland home games throughout the 1982-83 season and the early part of the 1983-84 season.

Aerial photo of ground circa 1983. Note the open unreserved terrace on the Olympia side, and the extension to the viewing lounge

The last large crowd to gather on the old terrace was for a benefit game for retiring IFA secretary Billy Drennan, on 3rd August 1983. Some 30,000 fans watched an enthralling match between the two most prominent English clubs - Manchester United (the FA Cup holders) against Liverpool (the League champions and League Cup holders). Man. Utd won 4-3.

Linfield had retained the Irish League title in 1983, and were drawn to play Portuguese champions Benfica in the European Cup. The home game on 28th September 1983 (Benfica, managed by future England manager Sven-Göran Eriksson, won 3-2) was the last at which the unreserved terrace was used. Work commenced the next day on the building of the new grandstand.

For the duration of the work Linfield fans on the terraces were confined to the Spion Kop. Linfield kept fans updated on progress with the construction

Work begins to remove the old terracing

of the new grandstand via the match day programme 'Look at Linfield'. In February 1984 it reported: 'The progress made in the erection of the new 6,800-seater grandstand is remarkable and it is expected the work will be completed in May 1984. During recent storms, damage to sections of the main grandstand was sustained and we apologise to those supporters who normally occupy Section F [nearest the "tunnel" at the south-west corner] for the inconvenience caused. It is the intention of the Management Committee to carry out major refurbishing and repair work on the grandstand in coming months so as to maintain the standards at our international stadium.'

Later that month the completion date had changed: 'The grandstand is scheduled to be complete [by mid-June 1984]. The extreme wintry weather conditions earlier this year did halt some of the work...but the contractors are confident of reaching a mid-summer completion date.'

Linfield match day programmes also carried an advert for the sale of 20-game tickets for international games, priced at £100 each, with an artist's impression of the new stand, to be known as the North Stand:

Artist's impression of the new stand

The North Stand design was undertaken by Ferguson and McIlveen, Consulting Architects and Structural Engineers, in partnership with the Scottish firm TM Millar and partners, with Thorburn Associates acting as specialist consultants and followed similar stands designed at Nottingham Forest's City Ground and Murrayfield, Edinburgh. They would later design four new stands at Millwall's New Den, which are virtually identical to the North Stand at Windsor Park. The total cost of the scheme, including professional fees, VAT, site investigation costs etc was just over £1.9m.

The government via the Department of Education contributed 50% of the total cost up to a limit of £1million. The Football Trust advanced £500,000 and the Football Grounds Improvement Trust £200,000 leaving a balance of around £250,000 to be funded by the Irish Football Association and Linfield. Much of the IFA's contribution was raised through the advance sale of seats, and the sale of advertising space on the stand.

Football matches continued to be played at Windsor Park during the construction phase. In December 1983, Northern Ireland played what was to be the last 'home' Home International fixture, against Scotland. The

Early stages of construction of the new North Stand

English FA had announced earlier that year that the 1983/84 tournament would be the last they would compete in. As it turned out, Northern Ireland finished top of the table and won the trophy outright.

Just less than 12 months elapsed from work commencing on the clearing of the unreserved terracing in October 1983 to the official opening of the North Stand on 11th September 1984 on the eve of the Northern Ireland

The new North Stand takes shape

A bird's-eye view of the new North Stand under construction

versus Romania World Cup qualifying match. The official opening ceremony was carried out jointly by Nicholas Scott MP, Northern Ireland Minister responsible for Sport and Dr Joao Havelange, President of FIFA, the world governing body of football.

The match programme for the match contained the following details:

> "Work commenced on site in October 1983 with the completion date last month [August 1984]. JMJ Contractors were responsible for the total management and construction of the new North Stand. No nominated sub-contractors were involved in this contract.
>
> The seating decks consist of a lower deck of 15 rows at an angle of 19° and an upper deck of 19 rows at an angle of 28°. The total length of the stand is 114 metres and it has a capacity of 6,844 seated spectators.
>
> The entire structure free spectator decks are protected by a cantilevered roof, each truss member centred at 6 metres having a clear forward span of 24 metres. The roof trusses are fabricated in weathering steel while the remainder of the steelwork is protected from the elements by a Metalife paint system. Half hour fire protection is provided to the internal structural steelwork only and is achieved by cladding the steelwork with 19 millimetre Monalux sheeting.
>
> The underside of the cantilevered roof is finished in colour fast coated profiled steel sheeting incorporating inverted ducts to house public address equipment, lighting and emergency lighting. The roof structure is finished at the perimeter with G.P.R. cladding panels.

> The upper seating deck is constructed of pre-cast concrete units, supported on raking steel beams at 6 m centres, all forming part of a conventional steel framed structure.'

The construction of the North Stand saw the loss of the old terracing at the corner nearest the Railway Stand, the area being left as a flat, tarmac area where mobile catering vans could park.

Prior to the North Stand opening, Linfield spent around £12,000 on improving both the Windsor Park and Midgley Park pitches. Linfield also announced that the main grandstand would in future be known as the South Stand and the capacity of the stadium would be reduced to around 30,000.

In what was to prove contentious in the next century, the contract between Linfield and the IFA for the use of Windsor Park for international games was re-drawn in 1984 for an astonishing period of 104 years, at a 15% rental. Although the precise details of the rationale for this extremely long contract period are hazy, it is thought to have been a condition set by the government as part of its contribution to the costs of building the North Stand.

The North Stand in place. Note the extension to the Viewing Lounge

The North Stand (upper deck only) was first used by Linfield supporters in the European Cup match against League of Ireland champions Shamrock Rovers on 19th September 1984. However there were early problems with how the stand was to be used by certain local visiting supporters, as Look at Linfield reported:

'The decision to place Glentoran fans in the new North Stand for today's game had nothing to do with the Linfield Management Committee. It was a decision reached by the Royal Ulster Constabulary as part of their policy to segregate Linfield and Glentoran fans during Big Two games and the move was strongly opposed by Linfield Football Club. We remain of the opinion that it is preferable for the segregation arrangements of recent years at these games to continue, with Glentoran fans being accommodated in part of the South Stand [Sections A and B, nearest the South-west corner] and in the Railway Stand and Reserved Section [of terracing in front of the Railway Stand and beside/below the Viewing Lounge].'

In 1985, Linfield installed new modern dugouts in time for the World Cup tie between Northern Ireland and England on 27th February. The dugouts cost Linfield several thousand pounds. Each could seat 11 people, and replaced the covered structures which provided only bench seats. They were situated back off the track surrounding the playing pitch and extended onto the reserved terracing.

The match against England was attended by a sell-out crowd of 28,500 – a good indicator of the ground's new capacity. Tragedy was averted when a terrorist bomb was detonated an hour after the match concluded at a petrol station on Tate's Avenue, a few hundred yards from the ground.

Linfield commercial manager Bertie Entwistle in the new dugouts, 1985

1985 - Bradford and Heysel

Just three years after the fire that destroyed the unreserved roof over the Olympia terrace at Windsor Park, a stand at the home of English Third Division club Bradford City, of similar vintage, built by the same designer (Archibald Leitch) and constructed from the same basic wooden materials, caught fire during a game, but with much more tragic consequences.

The Main Stand at Bradford City's Valley Parade was 77 years old and was being occupied for the last time on 11th May 1985 as workmen were due to dismantle its roof, made of wood and covered in tar - the work being needed as a condition to the club's promotion to the old Division Two. Some of the building materials had already been delivered and stored behind the stand in readiness for work to begin.

A crowd of 11,000 was in attendance. About 35 minutes into the game, a cigarette was discarded, and litter that had accumulated in voids under the stand's wooden floor ignited. Spectators watched and hesitated at first, and then belatedly fled the ensuing fireball. The wooden construction of the stand aided the spread of the fire and took the lives of 56 men, woman and children, with the whole event played out live to an appalled television audience.

Just a few weeks later, on 29th May 1985, 39 fans were killed and over 600 injured when a wall collapsed at the Heysel Stadium in Brussels, before the start of the European Cup final between Liverpool and Italian club Juventus.

In the wake of these double tragedies, local authorities all over the United Kingdom acted to prevent any repetitions. Windsor Park did not escape this and the Department of Economic Development's Health and Safety experts ordered the South Stand to be closed to spectators for an indefinite period from the beginning of the 1985/86 season, pending a consultative report. The decision did not initially meet with approval from Look at Linfield:

'The prohibition order on the accommodation of spectators in our South Stand has now regretfully been extended to the director's box and press box at Windsor Park, but our appeal against the Department of Economic Development's decision, allegedly taken in the interests of safety, will be heard on October 29 [1985] and we are hopeful of a satisfactory outcome which will involve the early return of fans to our main Grandstand. The inconvenience caused to our members and supporters by this prohibition is deplorable and with finance being lost to the club as a result every effort will be made to have the decision overturned. We would, however, point out that safety is always uppermost in our minds at Windsor Park and the necessary improvements will be carried out.'

Within a few weeks, the mood appeared to have softened:

'The Linfield Management Committee has submitted, through its professional advisers, proposals, which, if approved, would allow for the re-opening of the tip-up section of the South grandstand at Windsor Park, the directors' box, and press box...because of the colossal cost involved in bringing the entire South Stand up to the required safety standards the bench seat area will remain closed to spectators for the foreseeable future. The decision of the Department of Economic Development and the Northern Ireland Fire Authority is awaited and meanwhile we have postponed our appeal against the prohibition order.'

However, some months later the club again voiced its frustrations in a further match programme editorial:

'The obstacles we have to surmount to get our main grandstand at Windsor Park re-opened are unbelievable as over-zealous civil servants carry out to the letter of the law the stringent safety laws laid down after the Bradford City fire last summer.'

Decisions were, however, soon taken. In February 1986, the programme reported: 'Tenders have been invited for the demolition of the old Balmoral section of our South Stand at Windsor Park and we are hopeful that work will commence by mid-February [1986]...the non availability of the South Stand this season...has been a great inconvenience and frustration.'

By March, work was underway to bring the South grandstand up to the required safety standard. The first phase involved the demolition of the old Balmoral section that dated from 1929, and which provided seating accommodation for 2,000 fans. It was anticipated that when that was complete modern fireproofing, lighting and additional exits to comply with safety requirements would be installed, and the remainder of the South Stand re-roofed. The work was expected to involve considerable expenditure by the club and grants were forthcoming from the Football Ground Improvement Trust (£75,000) and the IFA (£50,000). The South Stand remained closed to spectators for the rest of the 1985/86 season.

With the Balmoral section now demolished, work continued prior to the 1986/87 season to enable the South Stand to re-open but with a much reduced capacity of 1,700. The old front row of seats was removed, and new exits constructed to the front and sides. A new roof was added, with the underside fire-proofed. All the bench seats were also removed and replaced with plastic tip-up seats, variously coloured blue and red. Also, the old divisions between the various "sections" of the stand were removed.

The work was completed towards the end of 1986. The reduced capacity of the South Stand led Linfield to appeal to fans: 'During recent games the

The Linfield grounds-man Harry Sloss in front of the partially demolished Balmoral Stand

South Stand at Windsor Park has been filled to capacity and for forthcoming games supporters are urged to come early to ensure a seat.'

The stand remained in this truncated form throughout the 1986/87, 1987/88, 1988/89, 1989/90 and 1990/91 seasons, with admission to Linfield games eventually being limited to club members and season ticket holders only. Other fans could pay at the gate for admission to the North Stand and Railway Stand.

Northern Ireland continued to play home matches at Windsor during this decade, though attendances began to fall off after the highs of qualification for the 1982 and 1986 World Cup finals. A World Cup qualifier against Malta on 21st May 1988 attracted only 12,000 spectators.

There were concerns of a different kind the previous year. On 1st April 1987, Northern Ireland played England in a European Championship qualifier. Less than an hour before kick-off, an IRA bomb exploded about 100 yards from the main entrance to Windsor Park, causing some damage to a garage and other property. Luckily, no-one was killed or injured.

Other improvements made during the 1980's included the provision of a "security tower", erected beside the player's tunnel, an electronic scoreboard on the Railway Stand fascia, and a temporary netting which was strung between six posts behind the goal at the Spion Kop end in late 1988. This was in response to bottles and other missiles that had been thrown from the Kop during Linfield's European Cup match against Norwegian side

England players check out the pitch whilst smoke billows from a bomb detonated close to Windsor Park, 1987

Lillestrom in 1987. That incident led to a further ban on European 'home' games, and in the following two seasons Linfield's European home legs were played at the Racecourse Ground, Wrexham, Wales.

The North Stand's construction did not please everyone, however. Residents living directly behind it, on Olympia Drive, found that the drafts it created down their chimneys made it almost impossible to use their fireplaces. In 1988, the Court of Appeal rejected a claim by Belfast City Council that alleged blow-down of smoke into 21 homes on Olympia Drive constituted a nuisance within the meaning of the Pollution Control and Local Government (NI) Order 1978.

14

The 1990s

Farewell to the Kop

The event that had the biggest impact on the stadium in the 1990s took place on 15th April 1989 at the Hillsborough ground of Sheffield Wednesday. Long thought to be one of the safest (and biggest, capacity-wise) grounds in England, it regularly hosted neutral FA Cup semi-final matches. On that day, Liverpool were drawn to play Notts Forest. A combination of poor design and ineffective crowd management by the police led to a crush on the terraces which saw 96 fans lose their lives.

The South Stand extension

The disaster led to an inquiry by Lord Justice Taylor, whose report made the significant recommendation that terracing should be phased out at the majority of grounds in Great Britain. The complexities of the constitutional arrangement whereby Northern Ireland was under 'direct rule' from the Westminster government meant the report's findings did not apply to Northern Ireland.

Separately, FIFA decreed in July 1989 that from 1992 no standing spectators would be permitted at World Cup qualifying matches. This saw the closing of the Spion Kop and reserved terracing for competitive internationals staged at Windsor Park from 1991/92 onward, though it remained open for Linfield games. Without the Kop available, capacity for international games was reduced to around 11,000, seated in the North, South and Railway stands.

The Troubles still cast a dark shadow over football in Belfast, and at a Linfield v Cliftonville match on 5th November 1991 a terrorist grenade was thrown from outside the ground into the area on the Spion Kop where Cliftonville's fans were gathered. There were no serious injuries.

At the start of the 1991/92 season Linfield announced new works, some of which were undertaken, some of which would wait for a few more years:

> 'Work will start in the New Year [1992] on a £1 million pound development at Windsor Park. An additional 1,350 seats will be erected with an extension of the South Stand towards the Viewing Lounge and 400 new bucket-type seats will be installed in the Railway Stand, replacing the existing 662 bench seats. It is proposed to erect seating at the Spion Kop end of the ground when the necessary finance becomes available.'

The extended South Stand was ready shortly after the start of the 1992/93 season. In essence, it was a continuation in design of the remaining 1930 South Stand. In hindsight, the more imaginative solution would have been to replace the entire structure. However, money was in short supply – Linfield's income from the rental of the ground to the IFA for international matches was decreasing as crowds dwindled. On 26th May 1989 a friendly against Chile was attended by only 3,000 spectators, incurring a £30,000 loss to the IFA. Competitive games fared little better - the Euro qualifying game against the Faroe Islands on 1st May 1991 attracted only 8,000 spectators; by the time of the match against Lithuania, on 28th April 1992, the crowd number had fallen to 5,500.

The first use of the newly extended South Stand was at the Northern Ireland v Albania match on 9 September 1992; Linfield supporters first had access on 12 September in a game versus Bangor, though the official opening took place at the Northern Ireland v Spain match on 14 October.

The end of the Spion Kop

The Spion Kop was doomed after the changes being made to football stadia across the UK. It was to have a last hurrah in 1996, when it was opened for the last time at an international match for a friendly against Germany on

WINDSOR PARK - A History of the Home of Linfield FC & Northern Ireland

The Spion Kop in the early 1990s

29th May 1996 (the Germans were using Northern Ireland as their training base just prior to the Euro '96 finals held in England that summer). The match ended in a 1-1 draw, with Germany famously missing two penalties (they must have practised thereafter as they went on to beat England in the semi-final of Euro '96 in a penalty shoot-out).

View of the last international at which the Kop was used, N Ireland v Germany 29 May 1996. Note the netting behind the goal, and the police security tower

The Kop terracing was used for the final time at a Linfield v Liverpool friendly on 2nd August 1996. Over 17,000 spectators saw the Blues earn a credible 2-2 draw. Construction of a new Kop Stand commenced shortly afterwards, and continued throughout the 1996/97 season.

The new stand cost around £2million. Linfield bore the brunt of the costs, though there were contributions from the Football Trust and the IFA. It had a capacity of around 4,000, and was opened on 26th July 1997, when Linfield again played Liverpool in a friendly match, the Reds winning 2-1 courtesy of two goals from 17 year old Michael Owen. The stand was similar in design to stands built at Kilmarnock's Rugby Park ground, and was quite

Bulldozers move on to The Kop

basic, consisting of two sections and containing no corporate facilities. As part of the construction process the floodlights at this end of the ground were moved to a position in each corner.

The new Alex Russell Kop Stand

In 2004 Linfield ran a competition for fans to name the stand, with the winner choosing to call it after Alex Russell, Linfield goalkeeper of the 1950s.

In the late 1990s the original yellow seats in the lower deck of the North Stand, weathered by the elements, were replaced with red seats.

WINDSOR PARK - A History of the Home of Linfield FC & Northern Ireland

A view from the late 1990s. The south stand has been extended and the new Kop Stand is in place, but the yellow seats in the lower deck of the North Stand have still to be replaced

15

2000s

Decline and renewal

The first decade of the new millennium was to see much debate, but little by way of action, about the future of Windsor Park. The first rumblings about its suitability as an international venue were sounded in August 2000, when Ernie Walker, chairman of UEFA's stadia committee, commented that facilities at Windsor Park would soon not meet the standard required for World Cup and European Championship games: 'There are parts of Windsor which are acceptable but the main south stand needs to be demolished, so too does that at the railway end and be rebuilt'.

The Railway Stand showing its age

In October 2000, Windsor Park was the unusual choice as venue for the opening fixture of the Rugby League World Cup, Ireland defeating Samoa 30-16 in a heavy downpour.

In 2001, an Advisory Panel set up by the Northern Ireland Assembly and chaired by ex-Linfield and Northern Ireland player Billy Hamilton, delivered the "Creating a soccer strategy for Northern Ireland" report. Amongst its many recommendations was a call for a 'National Stadium'. Such an idea had already been considered feasible under certain circumstances by a previous grouping (the National Stadium Working Group, set up under the auspices of the Sports Council in 1999). Although initially rejected by the Sports Minister Michael McGimpsey on the grounds of cost, which he estimated at £60m, the IFA and Linfield produced the "Vision of the future plan" that estimated a more modest-costing improvement. In September 2002 David Bowen, IFA Secretary, said 'in the absence of movement on the National Stadium issue, Windsor Park remains the most suitable venue'. The breakdown on the Windsor Park upgrade was:

- Refurbishment of North Stand, including replacement lighting, £300,000
- Replacement of South Stand £9.1m
- 1,000 square metre commercial office accommodation £900,000
- Changing pavilion at West Stand £380,000
- Provision of new pitch, including under-soil heating and sprinkler system, £750,000
- General site works, including turnstiles, £700,000
- Floodlighting £300,000
- NI Electricity upgrade £60,000
- General refurbishment £20,000
- PA system £200,000
- CCTV £250,000
- Preventive maintenance/diversions £200,000

In 2003, UEFA were expressing their concerns about the suitability of Windsor Park to host international games. David Bowen was again quoted: 'At the last match against Armenia, the doping control room and toilet facilities for players providing urine tests were unsatisfactory. There is a big danger that if Windsor is not improved, then we could be looking for another venue which would mean taking fixtures away from the province.'

Out of bounds terrace at the railway end

Linfield were struggling financially, partly due to necessary expenditure on facilities at Windsor Park such as drug testing and first aid rooms, press and media areas and so on, to keep it up to UEFA and FIFA standards. Revenue from the crowds at international games was on the low side, with average attendances hovering around the 7,000 mark. By late 2003 the club's overdraft had spiralled to £700,000, and the Linfield Committee briefly considered selling off the land at Midgley Park for retail development to offset the financial difficulties.

Linfield were drawing average attendances of around 2,500 although the occasional big game, such as the Linfield v Glentoran Irish Cup final on 6th May 2006, attracted a crowd of 12,500. Windsor Park had been decreed the venue for all Irish Cup finals from 1996, irrespective of whether Linfield were involved, and the Blues played the 2002 final against Portadown at the venue, winning 2-1.

However an upward change in the fortunes of the international side saw the "sold out" notices go up once again, most famously when Northern Ireland beat England 1-0 on 7th September 2005, with future Linfield manager David Healy scoring the winning goal – the first home victory over the English since 1927. 14,000 fans were present on that historic night. All told, the IFA paid Linfield £440,000 in the 2005/06 year – five times the amount paid in 2003. The club was also successful on the pitch, winning all four domestic trophies in 2005/06 along with the all-island Setanta Cup, and the increased revenue from prize money allowed the club to make significant inroads into clearing its crippling debt.

Also in 2005, a National Stadium for football, gaelic sports and rugby and situated on the site of the old Maze Prison, some 15 miles outside Belfast, was announced by the British government, as the Daily Mirror reported:

'The Maze jail site was last night identified as the only suitable location for Northern Ireland's new national sports stadium. Consultants assessing land where the notorious prison once stood declared the grounds had scored better than two shortlisted Belfast areas - the Titanic Quarter and North Foreshore. Reinvestment Minister Ian Pearson MP, who is involved with plans for a 30,000-seater arena, said the others were considered too expensive. He added: "Work is continuing in relation to the stadium and its viability, particularly in relation to getting agreement on the way forward with the key sports bodies in the coming months. We are now moving forward with this business planning work on the basis that we are only considering the Maze/Long Kesh".'

The IFA seemed "sold" on the idea of a new, National Stadium, and in January 2006 it gave its support in principle to the construction of a new national sports arena, with Chief Executive Howard Wells telling reporters 'we have agreed to work with the government to further develop the stadium project'.

The first signs that this would not be easily achieved were reported in the Sunday Times in May 2006, reflecting the Linfield Committee's concerns that the loss of Windsor Park as an international venue would be a breach of the lengthy contract signed in 1984:

'Linfield demands £20 million to break IFA contract. Linfield is threatening to hold up the IFA's plan to move international matches to the planned new Maze stadium. An official from the Department of Culture, Arts and Leisure has been appointed as a mediator. The government has drawn up a shortlist of three companies to evaluate the value of the contract to Linfield.'

Meanwhile, the general condition of the ground wasn't helped when severe weather at Christmas 2006 damaged part of the roof of the North Stand, and debris was strewn on the pitch. The IFA Secretary Jim Boyce commented 'We have been told...to either replace the roof of the North Stand or simply take it off. The estimated cost of a new roof is £350,000 and we simply don't have that sort of money'.

2007 turned out to be a pivotal year for the future of Windsor Park. Consideration of the multi-sport stadium continued to cause much debate amongst sports fans and local politicians, with strong views expressed on both sides. The return of a devolved Northern Ireland Assembly in 2007 after a hiatus from 2002 had re-ignited the debate and the previous announcement regarding the site at the Maze seemed less certain, with an increasing lobby insisting that any new facility be sited in Belfast city.

What was certain however was Windsor Park's continuing unsuitability to stage major games. A report commissioned by Linfield warned of a serious fire risk in the largely wooden South Stand, where smoking was still permitted. In February 2007, Linfield announced a smoking ban:

'The Management Committee has no option but to BAN SMOKING both outside and in the all areas inside the South Stand. This includes the Press areas. There are no exceptions. Failure to comply could have serious implications to the Club. Those needing to smoke during match time should transfer to the Alex Russell Stand. The Management is confident of the goodwill and understanding of our supporters.'

In March 2007 the Railway Stand was condemned and barred from future use following a Health and Safety/Fire Authority assessment. It was also reported that a fire engine was on stand-by behind the South Stand at each international game (though pointedly not at Linfield games).

The South Stand and reserved terrace

In April 2007 the IFA struck a deal with Sky TV that gave the subscription broadcaster exclusive rights to show Northern International games. The deal was reported as being worth £10 million over four years. This new income would benefit Linfield as it was to be included in the long-term rental agreement between the club and the IFA – which would continue to draw the ire of other clubs, and parts of the local print media. The IFA, too, were concerned and in July 2007 they wrote to Linfield to seek an end to the 1984 contract. Linfield's response was swift:

> 'In 1984 IFA and LFC agreed by way of a written agreement that all international fixtures would be played at Windsor Park from January 1983 until the expiry of the agreement in January 2087. On Monday 16th July 2007 the IFA, by a letter signed by its Chief Executive Howard Wells, purported to terminate the 1984 agreement with effect from 16th January 2008. The IFA, by the terms of its letter, appears to suggest that it is entitled to terminate the 1984 agreement on two grounds, namely:-
>
> 1. that the 1984 agreement is revocable by IFA without notice, and
>
> 2. that LFC has failed to comply with its obligation to ensure that the stadium at Windsor Park is maintained in good order, repair and condition.
>
> Responding to each of these, LFC's position is as follows:-
>
> 1. The agreement signed by both parties in 1984 is not revocable

by either party. Had it been the intention that either party should have been able to terminate the agreement prior to January 2087 the agreement would have provided for this by an express contractual provision to this effect. There is no such provision in the 1984 agreement.

2. LFC accepts that it has a legal obligation to maintain the stadium at Windsor Park in good order, repair and condition (as set out in the 1984 agreement).

LFC has complied, and continues to comply, with that obligation. In common with many stadia of a similar age, aspects of LFC's facilities inevitably require repair, upgrade and renewal with the passage of time. LFC has co-operated in every respect with the current review of the ground being undertaken by the Miller Partnership and awaits with interest the outcome of that report when it is issued in final form.

To say that the stadium requires instances of repair, upgrade or renewal is entirely different however from saying that the ground is not currently in working order, repair or condition.

Were there to be any genuine concern on the part of the IFA as to the state of the ground at Windsor Park it seems strange to the board of LFC that the IFA would have hosted an international fixture there as recently as 28th March 2007. Moreover, in its recent letter, IFA acknowledges (albeit with conditions attached) that it is prepared to countenance the holding of international fixtures at Windsor in August and November. Indeed, as recently as 18th June, LFC was happy to receive its UEFA license, which permits it to play matches at Windsor Park under the auspices of UEFA. One of the signatories of the UEFA license was in fact Mr Wells.

To date, and despite what it regards as considerable provocation, LFC has maintained a professional and non-public stance in its dealings with IFA. In light of IFA's purported termination of its agreement with LFC however, the board of LFC is reluctantly forced to conclude, and to state for the record, that it regards much of the IFA's publicly expressed concerns about Windsor Park as being motivated less by a genuine concern over the state of repair of the ground and more as the basis upon which the IFA now seeks to avoid its contractual commitment to LFC under the terms of the 1984 agreement.

It is LFC's informed view, as confirmed by its holding of a UEFA license and its insurers (who continue to provide cover), that the Northern Ireland team can continue to play at Windsor Park for as long as is required subject to the carrying out of those works which will be outlined and agreed in the final Miller Report.

Whilst, in light of IFA's recent correspondence, LFC has been left with no option but to refer this matter to its lawyers, the club confirms that it is willing and ready to explore and find a negotiated solution to the satisfaction of all parties; LFC does however expect the IFA (not least since it is the public face of the game in Northern Ireland) to act honourably and in good faith in its dealings with the club so far as the commitment it gave in 1984 is concerned.

In light of the fact that this matter is now with LFC's lawyers the club regards it as inappropriate to make any further statement with regard to this issue.'

The IFA issued a further letter in September 2007, again stating they wished to terminate the contract within six months, 'by virtue of the fact that Windsor Park has not been maintained in good order, repair or condition.' Linfield's further response was as robust as their earlier one, but this time took the form of a High Court writ:

'Linfield will further state that the grounds on which the IFA has purported to terminate the 1984 agreement are false and are made in bad faith, in order that:

(a) the IFA's desire to build a National Stadium and so fulfill its commitment to work with the government to deliver a new multi-purpose stadium without lawfully compensating Linfield for the termination of the 1984 agreement.

(b) the IFA can prepare a joint bid to co-host the UEFA Under-21 Championship finals in 2011, which requires an additional 20,000-plus capacity stadium.

(c) the IFA can solely obtain and use SKY TV contract monies, which may be available from January 2008.'

The situation was messy – not helped by an admission by the IFA that they held no documentation relating to the contract signed in 1984. In July 2008, the IFA president Raymond Kennedy had talks with former secretary David Bowen to try and resolve the matter, without success.

The proposed multi-sport stadium at the Maze was eventually ruled out in January 2009. Sports Minister Gregory Campbell, in a paper to his colleagues on the Northern Ireland Executive, ruled out the controversial plan for the site, opting instead to explore alternatives with the soccer, rugby and Gaelic Athletic authorities. Money was to be spent on an upgrade to Windsor Park so internationals could continue to be played there until a permanent solution was found.

Campbell set out the reasons for his decision, advising that the plan for the Maze site did not enjoy sufficient political consensus, and was too costly, an issue backed up by the business case drawn up by his officials. It was estimated to be a net loss to the economy of between £156m and £193m.

In September 2009 the IFA publically backed the refurbishment of Windsor Park, releasing the following statement:

> 'The Irish FA's Executive Board has agreed in principle to support the redevelopment of Windsor Park as the National Stadium for Northern Ireland.
> The size of the stadium, together with the ownership structure of the stadium and negotiations around the existing contract with Linfield FC were not discussed but the Association will now begin work on these areas and other key elements of the redevelopment project. At this stage no further comment will be made.'

The chairs of the 11 other Irish League clubs were incensed, and wrote to the IFA in October:

> 'The recent announcement that Windsor Park is to be upgraded and its capacity increased suggests that on a conservative estimate Linfield's rent is likely to increase by £100,000 per annum under the terms of the current contract. Also there could be additional income from hosting other events, all facilitated by this proposed enhancement etc. It is in our opinion, a blatant contradiction to fairness and equity, and an affront to the other member clubs to even consider any upgrade in light of the above and further compounded by an historic lack of transparency attendant with much of the 'special' treatment afforded to Windsor Park.'

One club, Glentoran, took the matter to UEFA, writing to president Michel Platini:

> 'You will see that the arrangement gives one club an overwhelming financial advantage and we, together with other clubs, contend that this is detrimental and provides for an uneven playing field. This sweetheart deal has increased dramatically within the last year because of a massive increase in TV revenues and only further compounds the competitive imbalance.'

Platini and UEFA chose not to intervene on what was seen as a domestic matter, but the issue was not to go away as future years were to demonstrate. For their part, Linfield announced an upgrade plan. Two options were presented – a "quick fix" refurbishment at a cost of £3m, and a long-term fix at a cost of £20m, to include new South and East stands.

16

2010s

A National Stadium at Windsor Park

The "quick fix" identified to bring Windsor Park up to the required standards was progressed in early 2010. In January, UEFA confirmed they would contribute funding of around €500,000, with the Department for Culture, Arts and Leisure in Northern Ireland also making a contribution. The works included a re-roofing of the North Stand and the creation of new safety exits. The re-roofing element alone cost £300,000 and took place over the summer months.

Re-roofing of the North Stand, 2010

In August 2010 demolition work on the now unused Railway Stand, the oldest extant part of the ground dating from 1907, commenced.

The diggers move in to demolish the Railway Stand

Throughout the summer there were lengthy negotiations between Linfield and the IFA designed to give effect to the IFA's support to revamping the stadium. In June, an outline deal was agreed that would see the existing 1984 contact for international matches, which still had 78 years to run, scrapped. The 15% of revenue would be replaced with an annual index linked rent payable to Linfield of £200,000. A stadium management partnership would be formed and efforts made to utilise the promised government funding to build a modern ground capable of seating around 20,000 spectators. Linfield would continue to own the land on which the stadium would be built, and the IFA would have ownership of the stadium buildings, and all subsequent maintenance costs. The proposed deal was for 51 years, after which the stadium would revert to Linfield's full ownership.

The Linfield membership were called to an Extraordinary General Meeting on 2nd July 2010 and backed the deal. Members supporting the deal accepted that Windsor Park badly needed upgrading and the deal would keep the club on a sound financial footing for decades to come. In turn, the IFA welcomed the decision: 'This is another important step on making the redevelopment of Windsor Park a reality. The Association will now meet with our partners - DCAL, Sport NI and Linfield FC to discuss the next step in this process.'

In September 2010 Linfield explained to supporters that new safety requirements for Windsor Park had been agreed with Belfast City Council. In order to comply with the Safety of Sports Ground (NI) Order, and to obtain the necessary Safety Certificate, the capacity of the South stand was reduced to 1,686. Some seats were removed to provide better access/egress and increase gangways, whilst others were retained but put out of use.

The loss of around 1,000 seats would be compensated at international matches by the provision of temporary seating for 1,780 in the area where the Railway Stand had stood, and around 1,400 seats on the terrace in front of the South Stand. Fans attending Linfield home matches had to obtain a ticket when entering or leaving the South Stand.

Temporary seats in place in front of the South Stand and on the site of the demolished Railway Stand. Note also the yellow netting in the South Stand rendering seats out of use

The temporary seats were installed in September 2010 and first used at the N Ireland v Italy Euro 2012 qualifier on 8th October 2010.

In December, the Northern Ireland Assembly Finance Minister indicated in a draft budget that £28 million was to be set aside for the revamp, and this was confirmed by The NI Executive in March 2011. In total, the IFA would receive £61 million for both the revamp, and for a sub-regional programme to assist developments of other football grounds and facilities; the other codes of GAA and Rugby Union were allocated funding for their respective grounds at Casement Park and Ravenhill, both in Belfast.

It was to be some time however before work would progress. There were some grumbles from other clubs on the allocation but in February 2012 the Premiership clubs gave their backing to the deal. Linfield welcomed this, pointing out in a Look at Linfield article in March 2012 that essentially all that had been set out by the club and endorsed by the membership in 2010 had now been delivered.

By July 2012 formal arrangements were being put in place to take the redevelopment project forward. The IFA were in the lead, and appointed Belfast-based firm Hamilton Architects to lead the integrated consulting team, which included the RPS Group, for what was now being referred to as 'Northern Ireland's National Stadium Project'. The aim was to draw up designs for an 18,000-capacity venue on the site of Windsor Park, with a planning application to be submitted by December 2012. Work was projected to commence in the summer of 2013, with the stadium completed by summer 2015.

In essence, the plans would see the removal of the South Stand and a new, integrated stand built on the site and extending to the site of the old Railway Stand, incorporating changing rooms, press and corporate facilities. The Kop Stand and North Stand would remain in place but seating would be reconfigured. New roof-mounted floodlights would replace the four existing pylons, and the pitch would be re-laid and under-soil heating installed. Other works would include associated safety and accessibility ground improvements, turnstiles, site works, and external lighting. The IFA would relocate their headquarters from their historic home on nearby Windsor Avenue to the new stadium, and offices and a shop would be provided for Linfield.

Work continued apace throughout 2012 with the necessary public consultations on the plans taking place. A testimonial game for former Linfield, Manchester United and Northern Ireland goalkeeper Harry Gregg, in May 2012, had already been used as a test event to assess the environmental impacts of crowds and associated noise levels on residents in the surrounding area. With all the process issues completed, a formal planning application was submitted to the Department for the Environment by the target date of December 2012.

Approval for the planning application followed in a near-record time of eleven weeks, being granted by the Environment Minister in February 2013, and all seemed set fair for tendering to commence to allow for a construction start date of September 2013. But a delay arrived from an unexpected quarter. Despite the previous agreement of the Premiership clubs to the revamp, Belfast club Crusaders FC began legal proceedings to challenge the government's funding. Leave to seek a judicial review was granted to Crusaders by the High Court in May 2013, the action being brought on three grounds: that the deal lacked transparency; that the money the IFA would pay to Linfield constituted State Aid under European Union rules;

and that the funding arrangements breached competition law. The third issue was rejected by Mr Justice Treacy but the first two were upheld.

The invoking of a possible contravention of EU State Aid rules had the potential to delay construction by 18 months. With the date for the judicial review hearing set for December 2013 it was imperative that matters were resolved in order that the complete funding package for local football was not jeopardised in any way. Crusaders, coming under some pressure from the football community and local media, agreed in July 2013 to withdraw their action in lieu of a funding package from the IFA to other Premiership clubs being agreed.

Separately, there were other delays. In July 2013 it was revealed that all tenders for the construction work had come in over budget. After a recalibration of plans, the contract was eventually awarded to Newry-based firm O'Hare and McGovern, and a revised date for commencing work was set for the end of the domestic football season in May 2014.

Before then, in March 2014 Linfield members agreed a Board proposal that would see the club sign up to a joint venture project with Belfast City Council as part of a major investment in its Leisure Transformation Programme, to develop and enhance the facilities around the new stadium at Windsor Park, transforming the area at Midgley Park into a major sporting and community hub.

The last Linfield home match at the 'old' Windsor Park was on 22nd April 2014 and saw the team defeated by old rivals Glentoran. Linfield produced a commemorative medal for their fans to mark the occasion, many of whom

The South Stand April 2014 – the last Linfield home game at old Windsor Park

were given freedom to roam round the old stands and take photos. It was also the last home match for charismatic Linfield team manager David Jeffrey after his seventeen years in charge. The last ever domestic game held at the ground was the Youth League Cup semi-final between Linfield Rangers and Limavady United on 5th May 2014.

Prior to its planned demolition Linfield offered fans the opportunity to purchase seats from the South Stand, with proceeds being donated to Linfield's partner charity the Northern Ireland Children's Hospice.

Work got underway in June 2014 and initially all went to plan – a construction base camp was built at the forecourt at the railway end and a new access road was built behind the South Stand and leading to the Boucher Road; the pitch was removed to facilitate installation of new drainage, under-soil heating and re-laying; and work began on the new East and South Stands. Opportunity was taken to level the new playing surface, the old 'crown' pitch having run downhill from the railway to the Kop end by about 0.8 metres height difference.

The first phase – the re-laying of the pitch, and Linfield's temporary offices. The Viewing Lounge has been demolished

The discovery of asbestos in the old South Stand put work on demolishing that section of the stadium behind by 16 weeks, with the construction team having to switch emphasis to demolition of the Viewing Lounge and the piling needed for the new East Stand. As the intention was that there would be minimal disruption to Linfield both on and off the pitch during the redevelopment phase, temporary offices were erected at the north-east corner.

WINDSOR PARK - A History of the Home of Linfield FC & Northern Ireland

The second phase – the pitch is ready for action and the South Stand has gone. Temporary dressing rooms are installed between the two remaining stands

While the pitch was in the re-seeding phase in July, it was necessary for Linfield to switch their two home ties in the Europa League qualifying stages, against Torshaven (Faroe Islands) and AIK Solna (Sweden), to Mourneview Park, Lurgan. Although temporary dressing rooms were installed at the north-west corner of Windsor Park it was also necessary for Linfield to play the first seven games of the 2014/15 domestic season away from home, returning to base for the match against Warrenpoint Town on 13th September.

By October most of the South Stand had been demolished, and work was well progressed on the new East Stand and offices. On match days, home fans occupied the North Stand and visitors the Kop Stand.

Preparation for Linfield's players was difficult whilst the training facilities at Midgley Park remained out of bounds due to the construction. Over the course of the 2014/15 the team used eight different venues for training, sometimes on grass, sometimes on artificial surfaces.

An international match took place in October 2014, against the Faroe Islands, but the game against Finland in March 2015 was to be remembered

Cracks in the Kop Stand

for the wrong reasons. The day after the match, cracks appeared in the Kop Stand, seemingly caused by disturbances whilst the site for the new Council leisure facilities at Midgley Park was being prepared – a site that was on the original Bog Meadows ground. The decision was quickly taken that the stand would have to be demolished as it was beyond repair, and it duly came down in the following months. Decisions were also taken to replace the stand with a new build, making three new stands in total, and the work schedules were adjusted to meet this new demand.

A more immediate problem for Linfield was the ground was now unusable as the temporary dressing rooms were deemed too close to the demolition site. The team therefore saw out the last two 'home' games of the 2014/15 season at the Ballymena Showgrounds (v Glenavon), and at cross-town rivals Glentoran's The Oval (v Crusaders).

N Ireland v Romania June 2015. The east stand is in use for home fans, with away fans in a portion of the under construction South Stand

The IFA, too, had issues – the season's climactic showpiece Irish Cup final was also moved to The Oval were Glentoran took full advantage by beating Portadown.

For the scheduled international fixture against Romania in June, the IFA made swift arrangements for existing ticket holders of seats in the now demolished Kop Stand to be re-allocated to seats in the new, East Stand, with around 700 away supporters accommodated in part of the new South Stand – despite neither stand yet being fully completed.

Linfield were able to resume training on the Windsor Park pitch in July 2015, prior to a Europa League against NSI Runavik. Construction work continued throughout the year and by March 2016 the team were able to use the new dressing rooms in the South Stand, and the new club offices and boardroom were opened in the East Stand. Fans returned to the South Stand in April, and work also commenced on replacing the Kop Stand.

New, slightly larger, seats were installed in the North Stand with the capacity reduced by a few hundred. These seats, and those in the new East and South stands, were coloured variously green, blue and white in a seemingly random 'pixelated' fashion. Also, two small stands were constructed to fill the spaces at either end of the North Stand.

By October 2016 the new stadium was complete, and the opening ceremony was performed by FIFA president Gianni Infantino prior to the Northern Ireland World Cup qualifying match against San Marino. A sell-out crowd of 18,234 enjoyed a 4-0 home victory at the newly-named National Stadium at Windsor Park.

WINDSOR PARK - A History of the Home of Linfield FC & Northern Ireland

17

2020s

A stadium fit for the 21st Century

The ground had seen considerable transformation in the 28 months prior to the official opening ceremony. No trace of the original Windsor Park remains, with only the 1984 North Stand retaining a link to the ground's previous incarnation.

The finished stadium and new Midgley Park

The new entrance at the railway end

161

On accessing the ground from the railway footbridge, spectators are greeted by the new railway end, housing IFA and Linfield offices and shops, as well as an IFA Education and Heritage Centre. It provides a striking entrance to the stadium, with the green, blue and white colour scheme used for the stadium's seating replicated in the cladding. New automatic turnstiles are installed around the ground, and the entrances for spectators at the Kop and Olympia Drive have been much improved.

Inside, the new East Stand is a single tier of 2,438 general seats with spaces for 41 wheelchair users and companions. One corner continues into the new South Stand, with the other containing a large, curved screen to protect fans from the elements.

The East Stand

The South Stand and its two corner sections house new dressing rooms (one set for Northern Ireland, one set for Linfield's use), gyms and conditioning rooms, media centre, corporate lounges and bars – all the requirements of a UEFA Category 4 stadium. It is also the location of the IFA's Education and Heritage Centre, part of which is a display illustrating the history of the stadium, including a scale model of the ground at various stages of its development.

There are 3,231 general seats and around 1,000 corporate/VIP seats on the main, lower deck. The upper deck consists of 1,080 general seats and around 200 press/media spaces. A large video screen/scoreboard is built in to the corner between the East and South Stands. The new stand can also accommodate 80 wheelchair spaces. Linfield have made use of the central corporate seats, making these available to around 200 supporters as Premier Seats, and the IFA sell corporate packages to international games. Stadium control facilities are built above the south-west corner section, which sweeps round to the Kop Stand.

The South Stand

The re-built Kop Stand holds 3,381 seats in a single tier, with the roof being an extension of that over the East and South Stands. It was built on the footprint of its predecessor so is set back a little further from the touchline than the other stands. The end of the stand has a similar side screen to that in the East Stand.

The Kop Stand

The revamped North Stand holds 3,450 seats on its upper deck as well as media commentary seats, and 3,017 seats on its lower deck. The concourse behind the stand has been covered over with a roof and new concession stalls created to sell food and drink on match days.

The North Stand

The rather odd new corner stands are limited in height so as not to interfere with natural light to the houses on Olympia Drive. Each is a standalone entity, and not integrated into the main stands on either side. Neither are they identical. The North West stand has 222 general seats and 12 wheelchair spaces, the North East stand 171 general seats.

The North West Stand, repurposed as a media centre for the 2021 UEFA Super Cup final

Buoyed by their on-field success under manager Michael O'Neill, which saw the international side qualify for the 2016 Euro finals in France, Northern Ireland fixtures at the stadium are invariably sold-out. The largest domestic attendance to date has been the 12,551 fans who attended the 2017 Irish Cup final, Linfield beating Coleraine 3-0.

The most significant match to be hosted at the stadium has been the UEFA Supercup final between Chelsea and Villareal. The IFA bid to host the game saw off rival bids from Belarus, Finland and Ukraine. For the match, played on 11th August 2021, the pitch was re-laid and new internal facilities (including for the controversial VAR system) installed.

Only two other sporting events have been hosted at the stadium – a motocross event in June 2016, and a boxing night in August 2018 featuring Tyson Fury and local hero Carl Frampton on the bill. The IFA do have plans to host major music concerts in the future.

Inside the stadium, viewed from the North-West corner stand

Midgley Park

The Midgley Park redevelopment project was completed by the Spring of 2018 and consists of a 100 x 60 metre floodlit 3G pitch (oriented 90 degrees from the original pitch), a 200 seat stand and a pavilion, all designed to provide a permanent training base for Linfield and a centre for the clubs' ladies and junior sides. The Belfast City Council element of the project includes the Olympia Leisure Centre with swimming pool, a new Olympia 3G pitch, a children's park, access roads with dedicated parking for the leisure centre and a separate 80 space car park at the Midgley site. New boulevard style access, named Windsor Way after a public vote, creates a vista up to these facilities.

The stand at New Midgley Park

To the future...

The sharing of the stadium between the National Association and the leading club side in Northern Ireland has not been without issues. What to call the stadium remains a point of some contention, the IFA's preference being for the official title of 'National Stadium at Windsor Park', with Linfield and its fans and many in the media referring simply to the abbreviated form of 'Windsor Park'. Initial plans to sell naming rights for the stadium have not yet yielded a sponsor, though the naming of individual stands has been purchased by a number of local businesses.

Identity, too, has been an issue – the permanent signage around the stadium reflects the Northern Ireland team colours, whilst more specific Linfield-related emblems have to be erected and then dismantled for each Linfield match day.

Some Linfield fans have questioned a perceived lack of atmosphere on typical match days, with the average home support of around 2,500 spread across the lower deck of the South Stand (and occasionally the Kop Stand), with visiting supporters in the upper tier of the North Stand. Some feel it is 'too big' for the Irish League, despite the 18,000 capacity being modest compared to the 58,000 capacity reached in the 1950s. As was the case from the 1937 enlargement, the capacity will almost certainly always be more than sufficient for Linfield's needs. The club does, however, have ambition to increase the home support by 5% year on year, and also to qualify for the group stage of one of the UEFA competitions. Should that happen, the prospect of a draw against some of Europe's biggest clubs could well attract sizable attendances. Perhaps the continuing upward trend in crowds attending local domestic games will also improve the stadium atmosphere.

Despite the concerns, there is no questioning the vastly improved levels of comfort and sightlines from the stands, the bar and catering outlets, the toilet facilities, and arrangements for those requiring the use of wheelchairs. Not many Linfield supporters at the start of the 21st century could have envisaged that on entering the ground they would take an elevator to an exclusive bar facility before taking up a reserved, padded 'premier' seat right on the half-way line – and all at a modest annual fee

Conversely, the stadium is invariably full for Northern Ireland's home games, with a terrific atmosphere generated by the Green and White Army, some of whom would question whether the capacity is large enough.

As per the deal between Linfield and the IFA the stadium will revert to Linfield's full ownership and management after the 51 years stipulated have elapsed. By then, Linfield hope to have established a soccer centre in the Belvoir area of south Belfast for its successful Academy. But Windsor Park will still be 'home' for the Belfast Blues.

Acknowledgements

The first time I attended a match at Windsor Park in 1970 my father introduced me to one of his friends, Christy Campbell, a former groundsman at the ground. In the following years I listened to Christy's stories about how the ground had changed and developed over the years. I also avidly collected any photos and other scraps of information relating to the ground as they appeared in the Linfield match day programme, newspaper articles and so on. Malcolm Brodie's book "Linfield - 100 years", published in 1985 to mark the club's centenary in 1986, proved an invaluable initial source of information.

When the decision was made in the 2000's to re-develop Windsor Park I undertook, primarily and initially for my own satisfaction, to organise all my collected materials into a chronology. The inspiration for this was drawn particularly from the excellent series of books by Simon Inglis on the history of football grounds in England, Scotland and Wales.

The advent of the internet, and especially online newspaper archives, has made the job of the researcher somewhat easier, but I am indebted to the staff at Belfast Central Library and the Linenhall library for their assistance on sourcing some less well known newspapers and periodicals, and the Belfast Telegraph newspaper and Groundtastic magazine for other source material.

The staff at the Public Records Office Northern Ireland were also extremely helpful in sourcing the original Linfield FC Management Committee minute books.

The support of the current Linfield Management Committee has also been most welcome, in particular that of Chairman Roy McGivern and trustee Dr Cameron Ramsey and their unstinting encouragement.

Many other individuals have contributed photographs, old match programmes, hints and tips and general encouragement and I thank them all.

Mick Blakeman
Dan Brown
Michael Cockcroft
Gavin Maxwell (photos of modern Windsor Park)
Peter Miles
Martin Moore
Aaron McVitty, Belfast Telegraph Archives
David Sales
Stephen Shaw
Merv Payne, Victor Publishing
Darren Topping

The Block Bookers and the Saturday Gentlemen – Colin, Hugh, Jim and Gareth.

Finally, thank you to my wife Joan and son Chris for their patience and understanding of my obsession!

Selected bibliography

Brodie, M. Linfield: 100 Years (Belfast 1985)

Brown, D. Every other Saturday (Croyden 2016)

Garnham, M. Association Football and society in pre-partition Ireland (Belfast 2004)

Gould, M. H. A historical perspective on the Belfast roof truss (Construction History Society 2001)

Inglis, S. Engineering Archie – Archibald Leitch football ground designer (London 2005)

Templeton, G and Weatherall, N. Images of Ireland – South Belfast (Dublin 1998)

Coyle, P – Paradise lost and found: Story of Belfast Celtic (Belfast 1999)

Moore, C - The Irish Soccer Split: A Reflection of the Politics of Ireland? (Leicester 2020)

About the author

Joe Cassells attended his first Linfield match at Windsor Park with his father in 1970 at the age of eight years old. Football – and especially Linfield Football Club – was in his blood, his father having told him stories of watching the famous teams and players from the 1930's and his grandfather having owned a general shop on the Donegall Road in Belfast, close to both the Linfield Mill and Windsor Park and called, appropriately, the Linfield Stores.

That first visit sparked a lifelong interest in the design, layout and construction of Windsor Park, and this publication is the culmination of years of research into the ground, as well as the original homes of Linfield at The Mill, Ulsterville and Balmoral.

Joe is a Member of Linfield FC and regularly attends games home and away. He has also attended all but ten Northern Ireland international fixtures played at Windsor Park since 1971.

Got a book in *you?*

Victor PUBLISHING

This book is published by Victor Publishing.

Victor Publishing specialises in getting new and independent writers' work published worldwide in both paperback and Kindle format.

We also look to re-publish titles that were previously published but have now gone out of circulation
or off-sale.

If you have a manuscript for a book (or have previously published a now off-sale title) of any genre (fiction, non-fiction, autobiographical, biographical or even reference or photographic/illustrative) and would like more information on how you can get your work published and on sale in print and digitally,
please visit us at:
www.victorpublishing.co.uk
or get in touch at: enquiries@victorpublishing.co.uk

Printed in Great Britain
by Amazon